AlliedWorks Architecture

AlliedWorksArchitecture

Dwelling

Rizzoli
New York

New York · Paris · London · Milan

"Dwelling is not primarily inhabiting but taking care of and creating that space within which something comes into its own and flourishes. We do not dwell because we have built, but we build because we dwell."

—Martin Heidegger

08

Land, Light, and Craft

——Brad Cloepfil

←

Altered landscape: stone paddocks, Aran Islands, Ireland

We all seek a sense of home, a place to dwell on the land or in the city. We choose a house or an apartment that reflects who we are personally, culturally, and economically, then begin to occupy it with our families and possessions. Beyond mere shelter and protection, we seek places with "character or history." Yet in our culture of commodity, homes are more often a collage of hyper-stylized images and materials representing contemporary or historicist stereotypes, ephemeral and interchangeable—placeless, in history or on the land. Against this context of style and consumerism, a dwelling can offer a rampart of timelessness, something constant. A true home creates a location of reference and return, a link to history and an amplifier of context—a place that manifests memory. When all else is in flux, we aspire to connect to something that endures—a true there, there. In this context a home can literally create "time out," an interval of time and place against which the rest of our daily lives are measured.

←

"Hospitality consists in a little fire, a little food, and an immense quiet."
——Ralph Waldo Emerson

Mihalyo Daniel
from *Wood Burners*, 1997

As such, houses become vessels for rituals of occupation. A home accommodates acts both social and individual. We extend an invitation out to others, to cook and eat with us, a social signal of our cultural intentions. Yet we also gather in a place of refuge, we can find ourselves —a space of introspection, an inward lens that can reflect back out to the world. We look for renewal in rituals of bathing and sleeping. We create gardens as microcosms of the greater world, and burn fire, an archetype, for mesmerism as much as heat in a structured search of a connection to the eternal.

In our houses we are afforded control, a freedom of choice, and therefore we express our own sense of economy—economy in what and how much we choose to include, i.e., furniture and decorative and fine arts that communicate our cultural intention in dwelling. We curate our homes. Then, in determining the materiality of the house in the elements of making, we exhibit an economy of execution and craft. Attention to detail, the material things we assign value to all expressions of our personal ethics.

←

Allied Works Architecture
Case Work: Studies in Form, Space, and Construction. Toolbox Detail

Houses made with intention resonate with a particular place, with the individuals who inhabit them and with the world around them. When considered carefully—in specific response to their surroundings, as amplifiers of light and space, with considered construction executed with care—a dwelling can bind us to the world, establishing a personal domain that filters the outside world, strengthening our sense of self, and, at best, nurturing our souls.

Land—
Siting and Bridging

"Once in his life a man ought to concentrate his mind upon the remembered earth. He ought to give himself up to a particular landscape in his experience; to look at it from as many angles as he can, to wonder upon it, and dwell upon it." ——N. Scott Momaday

←

Sun Valley Residence
Ketchum, Idaho

A house can enhance and interpret the possibilities of the land. The character and topography of the landscape and the surrounding planting and orientation provide an opportunity for a house to be absolutely specific, to be rooted. A dwelling can create its own ecosystem, as specific to a location as lichen on the north face of a stone.

We use two primary tools to engage in this larger conversation of location. The first is the development and choice of a site. Siting a building is not merely a matter of choosing a pleasing location. It is accessing and responding to the primary forces of a place—the scale of the landscape, the direction of the sun, the approach, the prospect—all of the qualities and character offered by the context. A rise of the land, a copse of trees referencing a distance view, the story told in the approach—all help the transition between the greater world and the inner home.

For Allied Works it is structure that forms the bridge from the city or landscape to prepare the ground for dwelling. The scale of structure mediates between enormity and intimacy, setting the domain that affords opportunities of privacy and occupation.

↑

Dutchess County Guest House
Stanfordville, New York

↑

Portland Heights Residence
Portland, Oregon

Life— Light and Space

"Insofar as we appreciate order, it is when we perceive it as being accompanied by complexity, when we feel that elements have been brought to order that windows, doors and other details have been knitted into a scheme that manages to be at once regular and intricate."
——Alain de Botton

⟵

Portland Heights Residence
Portland, Oregon

If landform and structure hold us to a site, it is light that brings the space of a house to life. Rooms become the amplifiers of light and are transparent and boundless, or controlled and intimate. The scale and proportion of rooms provide orientation and reference for the body to create the inherent qualities of a house. Proportion is the fit of a house, corresponding to the activities of public and private spaces. The senses of calm solitude or anticipation of celebration and invitation are generated by the spatial qualities of a place. Held in the world by structure, rooms envelop and secure a domain with the emotional play of light on surfaces. Beautiful rooms are where we want to dwell, to spend time, to invest our lives. They create the places of intimacy while communicating an invitation to the outside world.

Landscape rooms are a critical part of this celebration of life. The connection and extension of the house to the near ground, to gardens, terraces, and courts knit the dwelling back to the city and landscape. This middle ground is critical to our sense of location and place, a way of reforming the natural and urban worlds around us.

↑

Tribeca Residence
New York, New York

↑

Sun Valley Residence
Ketchum, Idaho

Craft—
The Hand and the Eye

"For my own part I am pleased enough with surfaces—in fact they alone seem to me to be of much importance. Such things for example as the bark of a tree, the abrasion of granite and sand, the plunge of clear water into a pool, the face of the wind—what else is there? What else do we need?"——Edward Abbey

←

Dutchess County Guest House
Stanfordville, New York

Houses are one of the few building types that exist at once in the immense and the intimate—existing on a larger site and within a more contained structure—but also in the details of construction, in cabinetry, and in furnishing. The choice of materials, the intention and care of construction as expressed in craft and joinery, create a conversation for the eye and hand. The visceral sense of house, its surfaces, its sense of weight or transparency—whether polished wood, raw stone, steel, concrete, or glass—create moments for the eye and hand to linger. Craft endures. It is a universal quality that imbues a home with value beyond the current occupant. Craft is a commitment to establish not only a home, but place in history—a demonstration of what we value in the places that we want to be in.

Furniture and decorative arts are a critical part of the conversation of the hand, eye, and body with the surrounding built environment. Just as beautiful museum galleries anticipate the art that will occupy its walls, a house isn't complete without the objects of occupation. The chairs and beds, lamps and tables extend the conversation of dwelling conceived by the architecture. They enhance its sense of context. The placement of a nineteenth-century writing desk in a twenty-first-century house, whether a family heirloom or a thrift store find, provides a depth of experience that amplifies the architecture, its character and its voice.

←

Blue Lake Residence
Sisters, Oregon

→

Dutchess County Main Residence
Stanfordville, New York

Dwellings

Dutchess County Guest House

Stanfordville, New York

Site Plan

The guest house was the first piece of architecture to be constructed on a large pastoral estate in Dutchess County, New York. The main residence, private art gallery, and outbuildings soon followed, along with the clients' diverse collection of site-specific contemporary art. The entire ensemble of buildings and art form a retreat for a Manhattan family who frequently entertain visiting groups and artists.

Balanced on the slopes above Ryder Creek, the house is woven into a mature forest of oak, hickory, and birch. It is a place of silence, reflection, and intimacy, reached by a raised path scored with the words of poet and artist Lawrence Weiner. The house is defined by a continuous, blackened steel frame that meanders through the woods and understory, blurring the boundaries between forest and dwelling. Panels of mahogany and floor-to-ceiling glass slip between, over, and through the frame, enclosing the rooms, framing views, and leaving open terraces. The house amplifies the calm of the forest, creating a framework for the changing seasons.

Floor Plan

—

a. foyer
b. living room
c. kitchen
e. bedroom
f. terrace

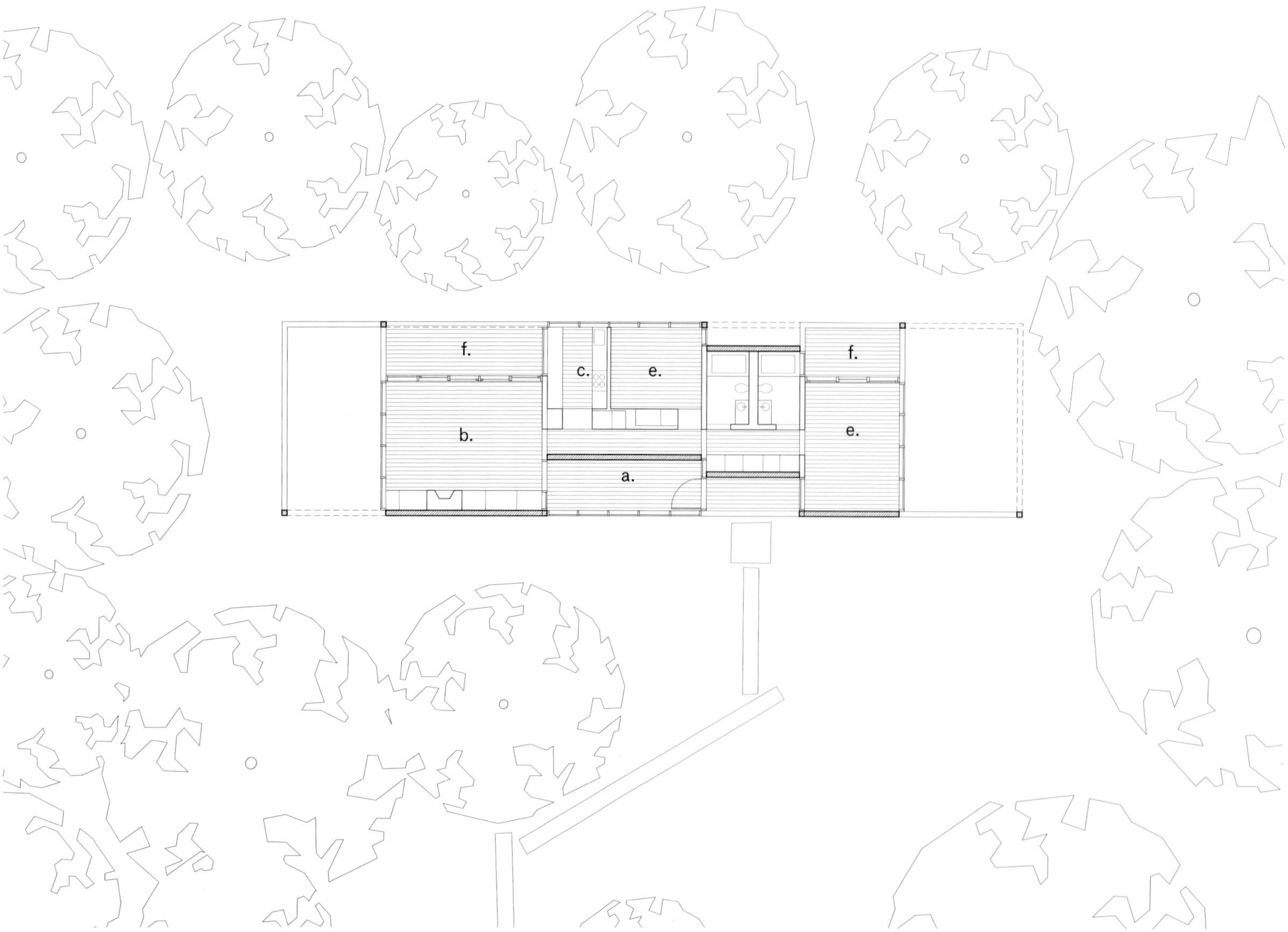

Sun Valley Residence

Ketchum, Idaho

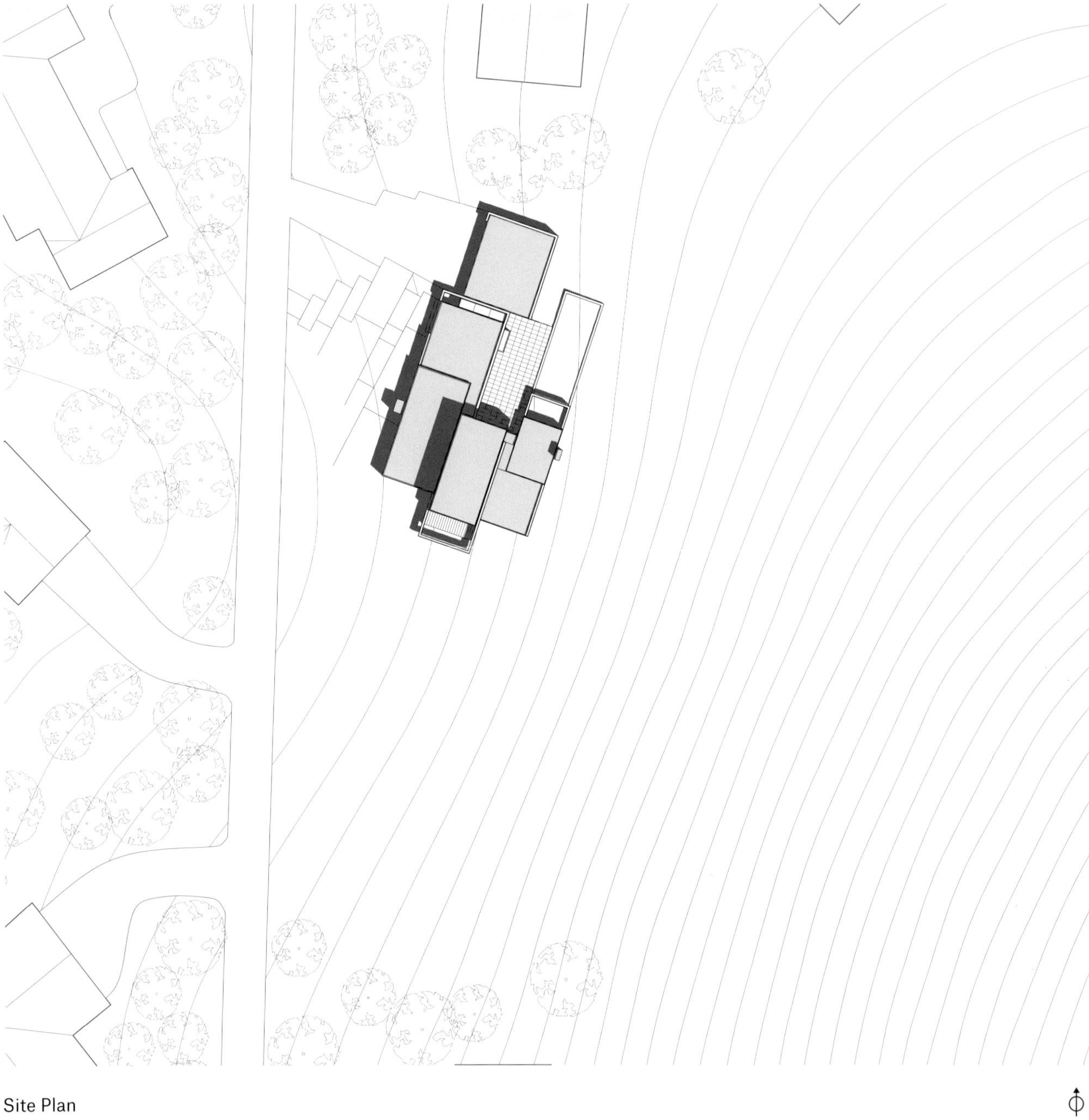

Site Plan

The Sun Valley Residence is a retreat for a San Francisco–based arts patron and her extended family. The client asked for an intimate and private house, a quiet and contemporary work of architecture. Located at the base of Penny Hill in an older residential neighborhood, the house is designed to frame views of the Sawtooth Mountains and the surrounding native meadows.

Built of meandering, plaster-like concrete walls, the residence nestles into the land's gentle slope and opens specific views out while providing screening from the street and adjacent properties. Offering privacy and connection from bedrooms and dining areas, the smooth walls slip seamlessly from interior to exterior, defining terraces and secluded garden courts, with views from the living room extending out to the mountains. All of the rooms are simple and elegantly proportioned, creating calm surfaces and spaces for artwork, while ensuring a warm and welcoming atmosphere.

Second Floor

—

e. bedroom

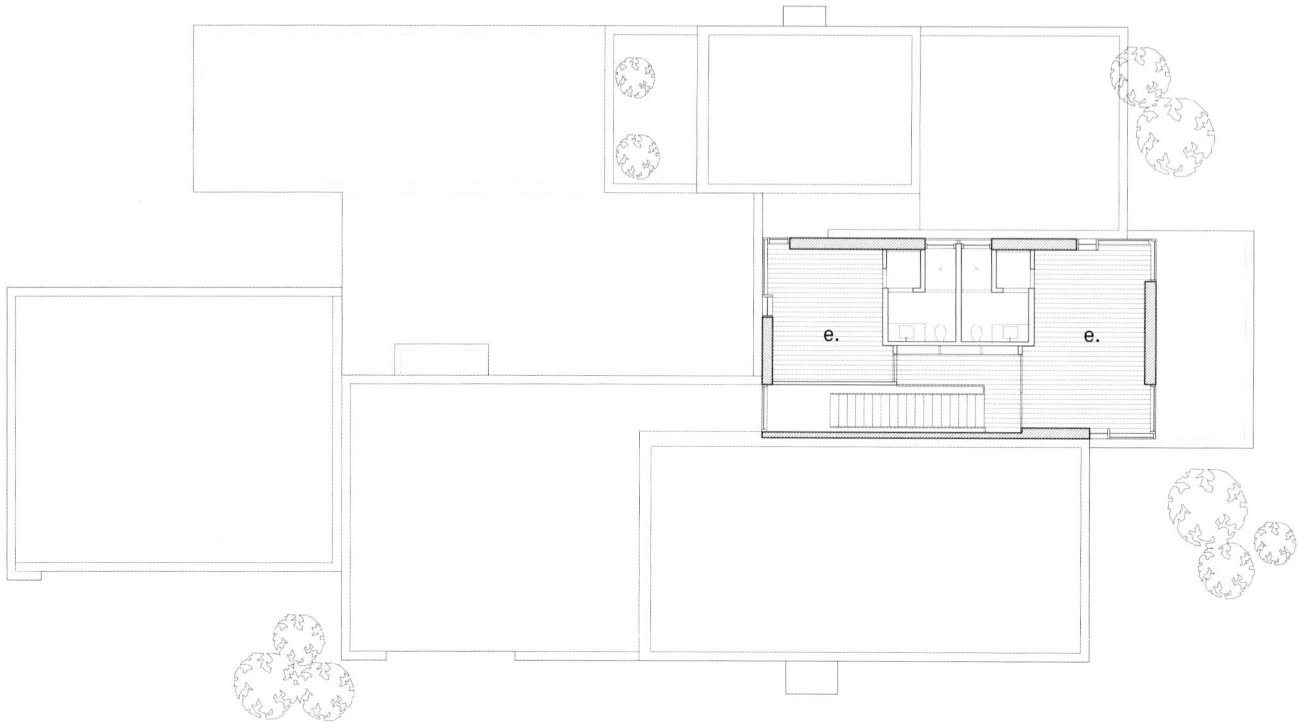

First Floor

—

a. foyer
b. living room
c. kitchen
d. dining
e. bedroom
f. terrace
g. master suite
h. garage

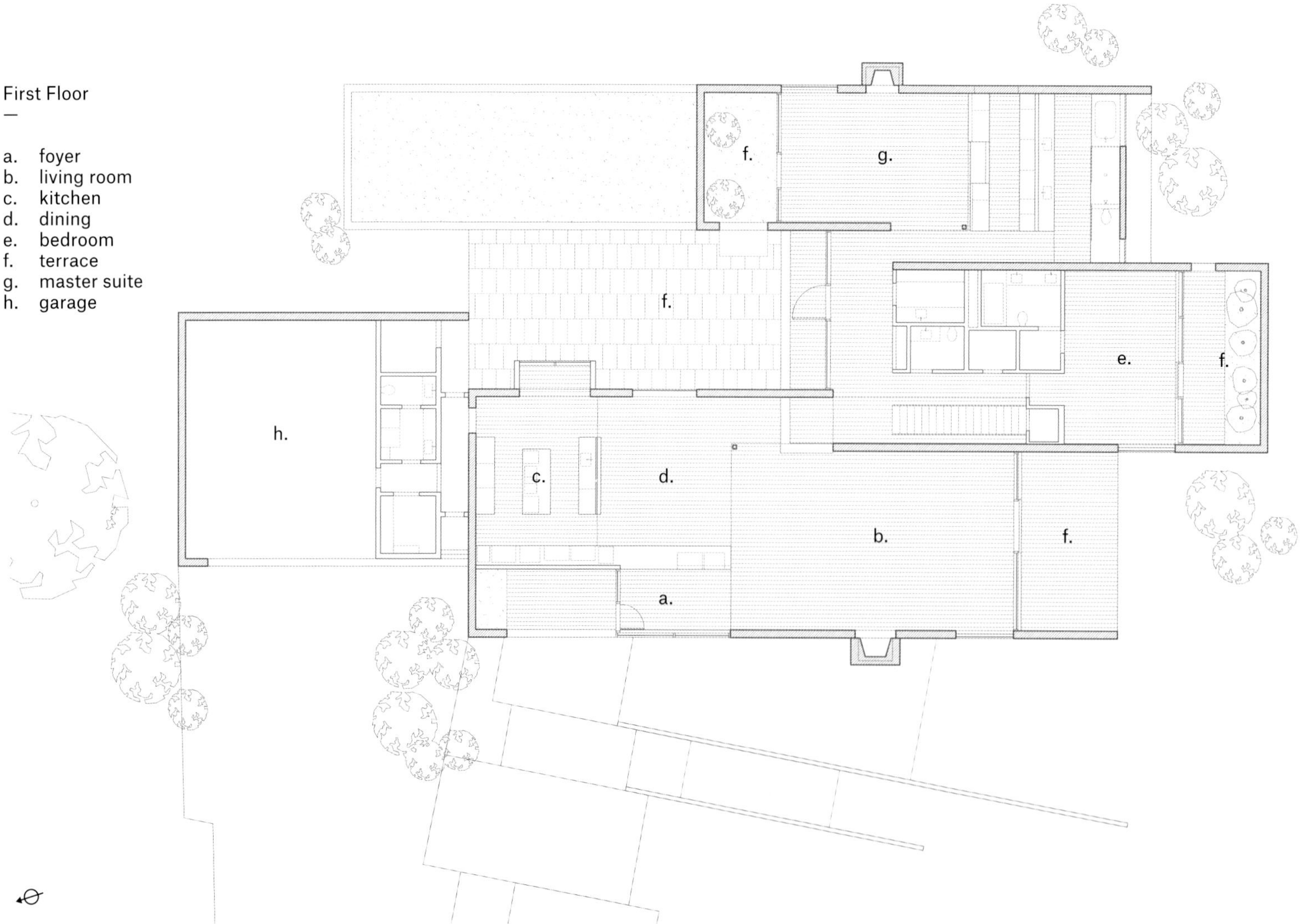

Maira Kalman
Summoning Ghosts: The Art of Hung Liu
WK5
HIMALAYA
WILLIAM KENTRIDGE TAPESTRIES
THE ART OF RICHARD TUTTLE
FRAGILE
Buffett

←

Ned Kahn
Kinetic screen installation, 2012

Neskowin Beach House

Neskowin,
Oregon

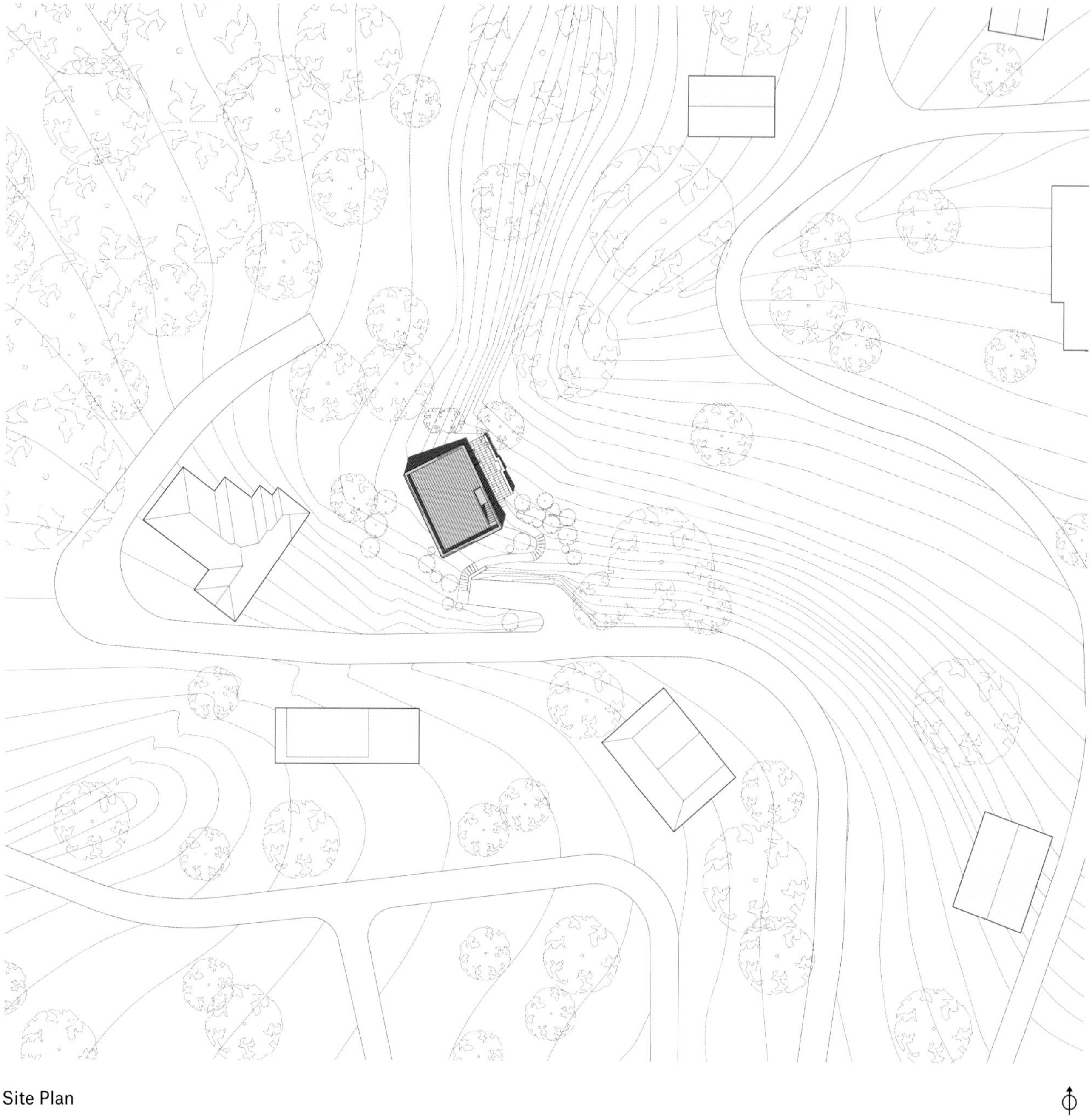

Site Plan

The Neskowin Beach House is located on a wooded hillside above a dramatic stretch of Oregon's Central Coast. Designed for an executive at Nike, a poet, and their family, the house is built to take advantage of sweeping views of the surrounding wetlands, forests, and pristine beaches. It is a true writer's retreat, offering space for work in solitude.

The compact three-level home is carefully crafted of cedar, hemlock, and plaster, with subtle modulations that orient to light and the landscape. Unified within and without by a shifting board-and-batten pattern, the house reads as a tower, with specifically sized and proportioned apertures precisely tuned to their orientation. Inside, a double-height living room, open kitchen, and dining space form the heart of the residence, framed by upper-level bedrooms and study, each with their own unique landscape views. Exterior stone terraces extend the living space and create gathering places within the steeply sloping site. Above, a rooftop belvedere provides 360-degree views and a place to fully experience the sea and seasons.

Second Floor

—

e. bedroom

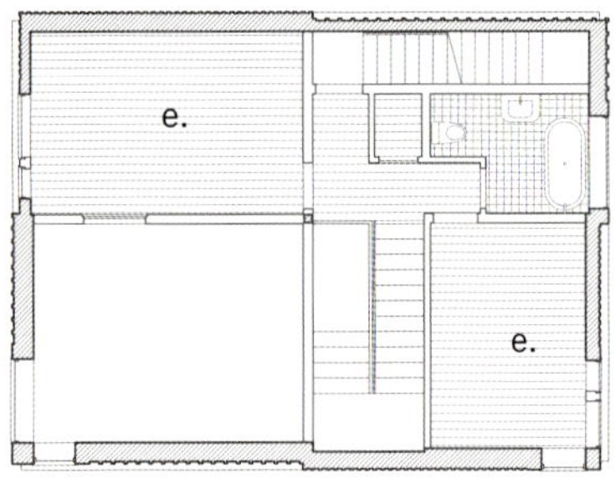

First Floor

—

a. foyer
b. living room
c. kitchen
d. dining
e. bedroom
f. terrace

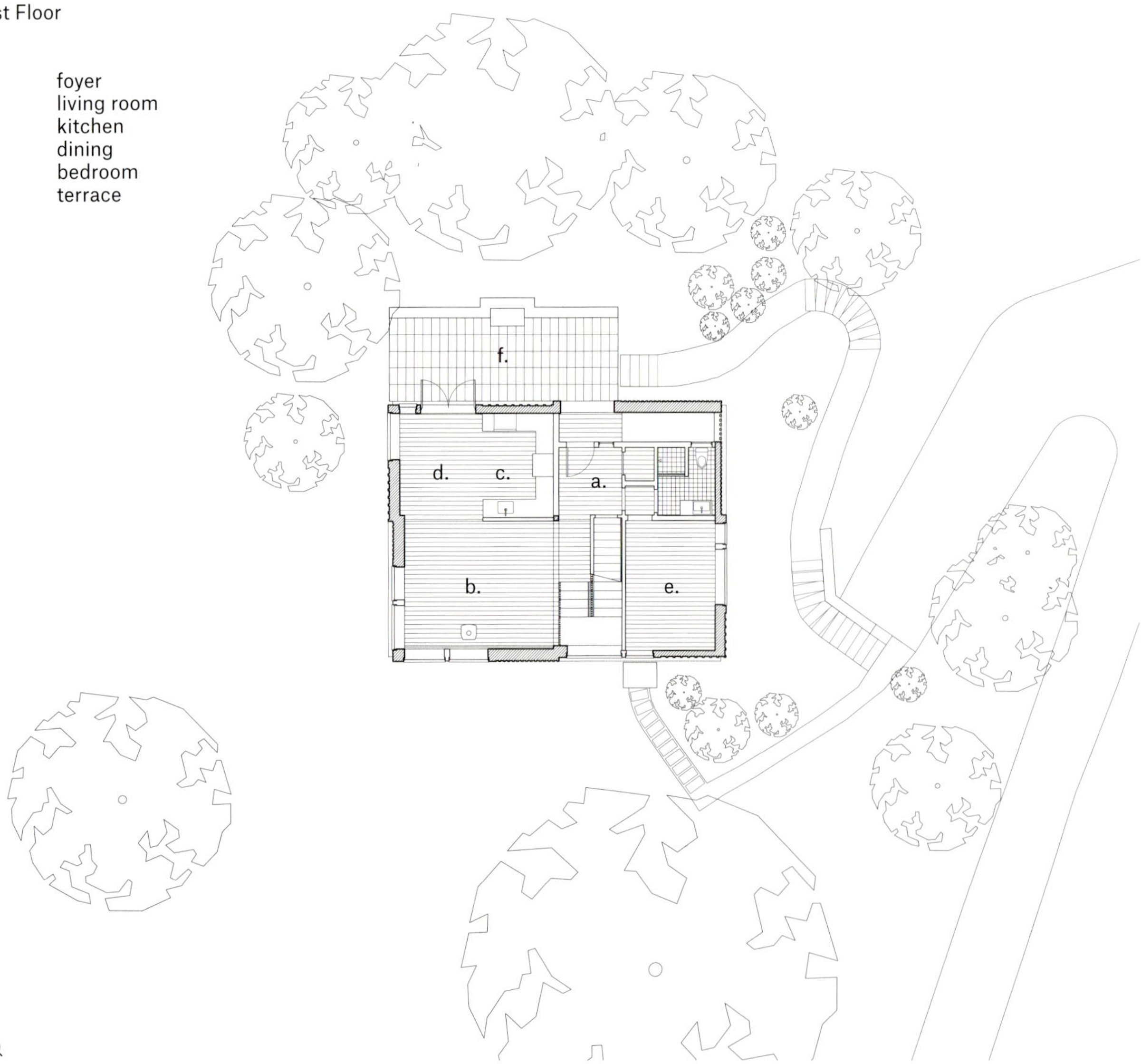

Willapa Bay Residence

Ocean Park, Washington

Site Plan

The Willapa Bay Residence was commissioned by a museum director and her partner, an accomplished photographer. The house marked a return to the Pacific Northwest for the clients, first as a summer home and more recently as a permanent residence. The property is on the remote Long Beach Peninsula in Washington State, looking across Willapa Bay and the Coast Range beyond. As a long-term residence and creative workspace, the house unites distinct spaces for living and work with the subtle tidal cycles and changing light of the bay.

Crafted of local Douglas fir, the house floats above the bay-shore wetlands, arranged as three elevated wooden platforms. Deeply overhanging roofs offer protection from the persistent coastal rain. On the first platform, the photography studio and garage serve as the gateway to the site. From this point of entrance, a raised board-walk traverses a sheltered garden and leads to the main house. An entry foyer, service spaces, and open kitchen are located on the second platform, which serve as a threshold to the main body of the house. On the third platform, a suite of bedrooms and dining and living spaces follow the water's edge, united by a broad terrace.

First Floor

—

a. foyer
b. living room
c. kitchen
d. dining
e. bedroom
f. terrace
g. master suite
h. garage
i. studio

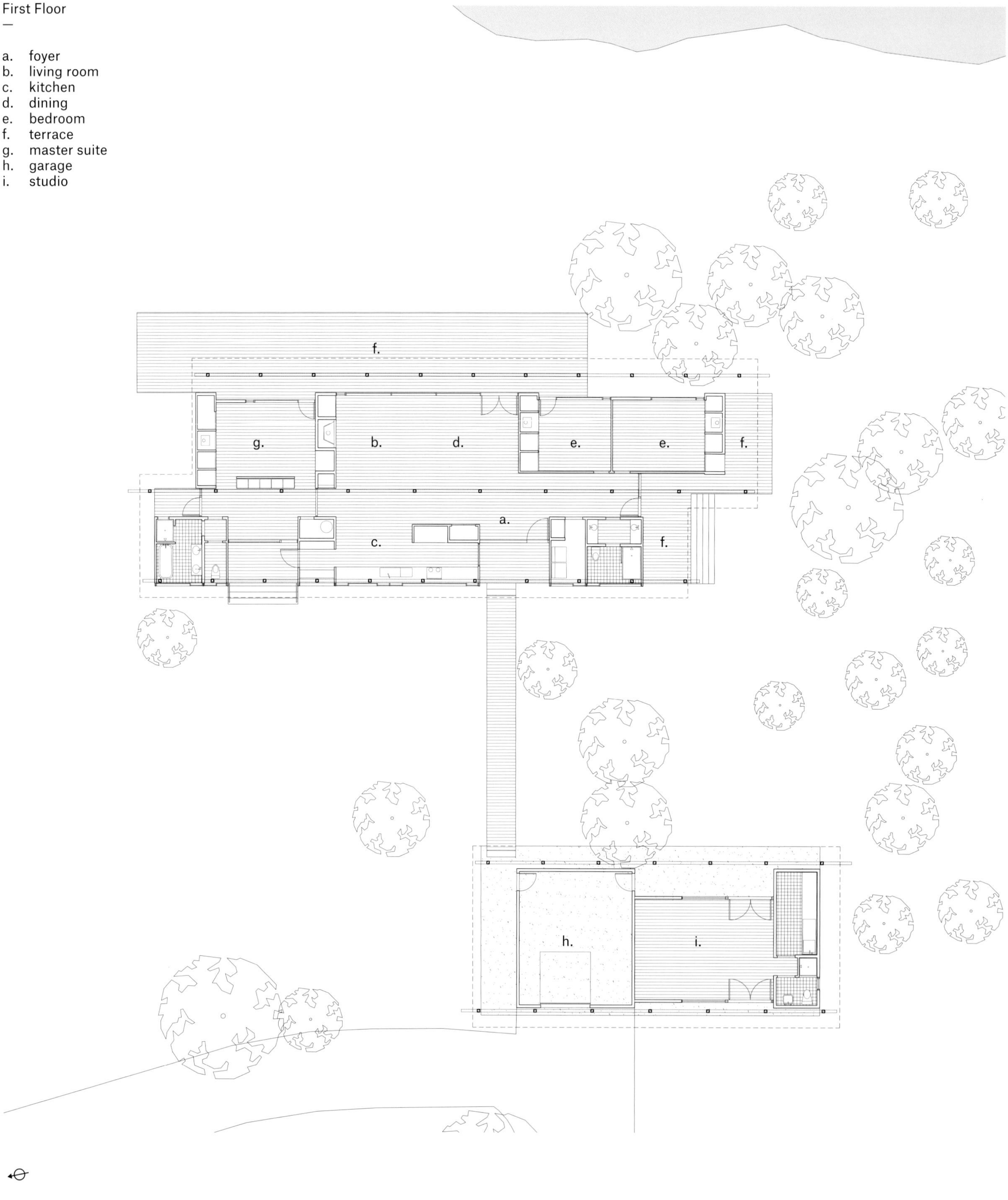

Glisan Street Residence

Portland, Oregon

Dosha

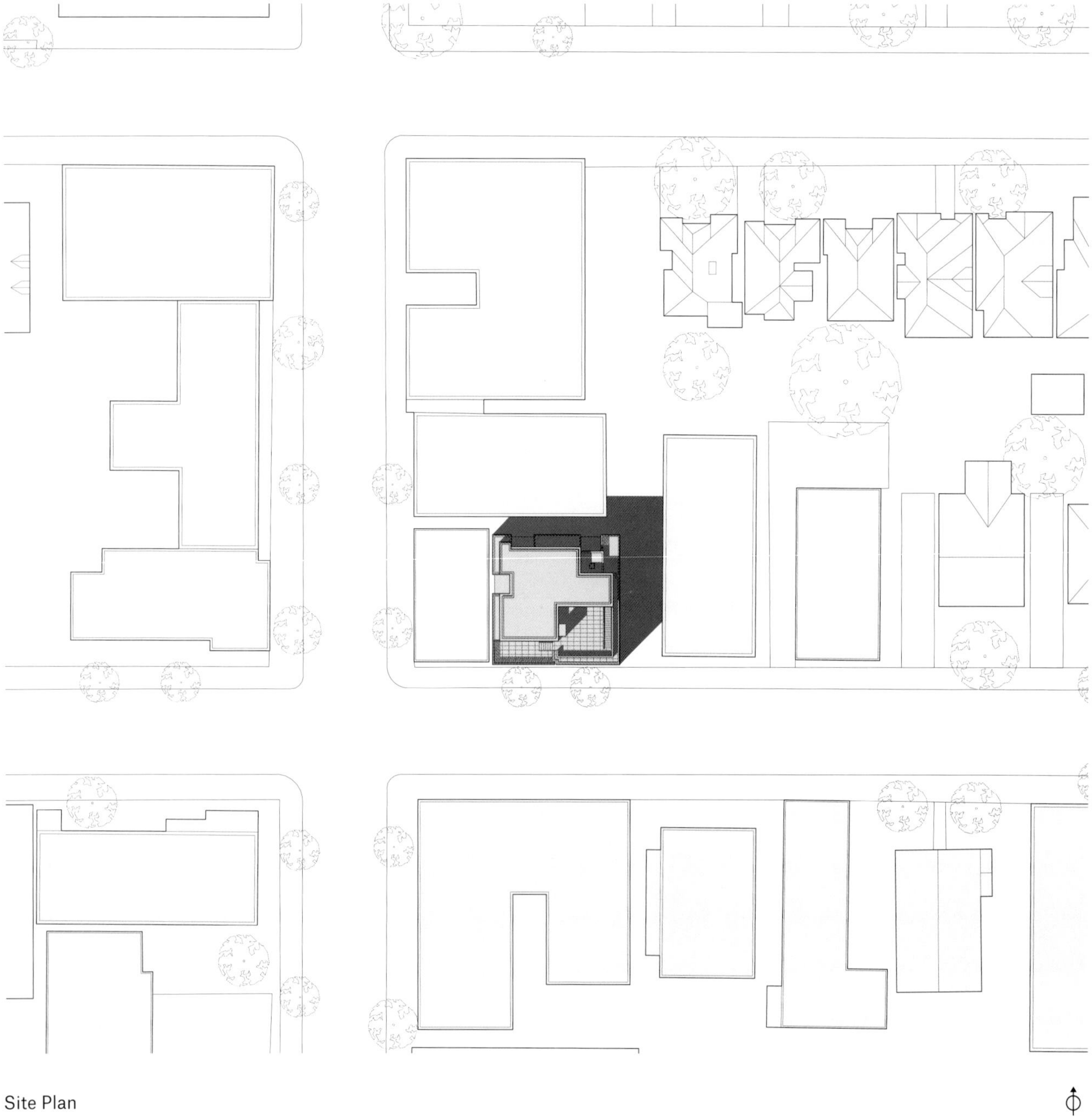

Site Plan

2261

2281 Glisan is a mixed-use building located in the heart of the Alphabet District, one of the oldest retail and residential neighborhoods in Portland. Built for a local developer and proprietor of a national tile and stone supplier, the structure combines commercial spaces on the lower three floors with a multilevel private residence and roof garden above. The residence provides a modest and efficient urban home after the couple relocated from a larger residence outside the city center.

Collectively, 2281 Glisan is a simple, elegant, and contemporary urban building of stone, glass, and stainless-steel mesh. A side setback for parking and loading access allows for uninterrupted light and views to the south and east. The composition of surfaces on these facades—solid, screened, and transparent—presents a unified exterior expression while negotiating diverse interior functions. Within the residence, a minimal palette of wood, plaster, and stone create a neutral field for the client's collection of art and furnishings. On the main floor, the open plan pinwheels around a central hearth, with living room, terrace, dining space, and kitchen following the open facades; above, a master suite and multilevel roof terrace provide a quiet refuge and place to view the city and the West Hills beyond.

Penthouse

—

e. bedroom
f. terrace
g. master suite
j. gallery

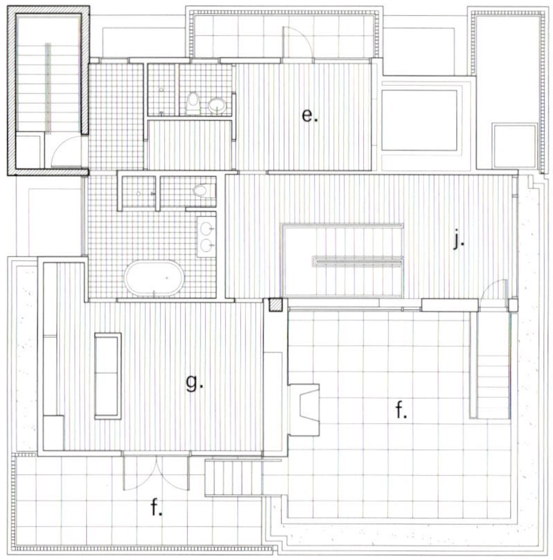

Fifth Floor

—

a. foyer
b. living room
c. kitchen
d. dining
e. bedroom
f. terrace

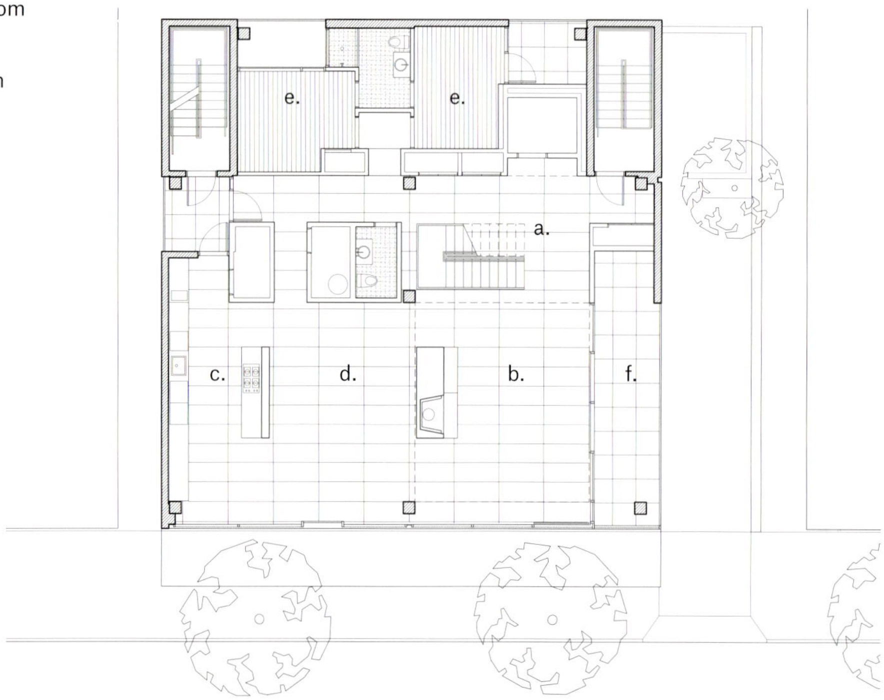

Blue Lake Residence

Sisters, Oregon

Site Plan

The Blue Lake Residence, designed for a renowned advertising executive and his family, is located adjacent to a remote volcanic lake in the Cascade Range of central Oregon. The residence was built as a retreat from the city while offering the flexibility to serve as a meeting place for their business and non-profit interests. The client asked for a home that manifested the historic materials of the mountain West: elegantly detailed, elemental, and at one with the land.

The house is set among the pines, overlooking the deep blue waters of the caldera. Stone exterior walls of local lava rock create the primary enclosure that protects the site and orients the house toward the lake. A heavy timber frame of entirely reclaimed Douglas fir lifts the roof that overhangs the stone walls and courtyard, protecting the house from heavy winter snowfall. A guest suite and utility level below the main floor and a two-bedroom loft accommodate both family stays and additional visitors. The main body of the house—comprised of open kitchen and dining areas, living room, office, and master suite—surrounds the courtyard, opening to the south with expansive glass wall panels and wood ventilation shutters. The entire house is a finely crafted piece of heavy timber cabinetry.

Second Floor

—

a. foyer
b. living room
c. kitchen
d. dining
e. bedroom
f. terrace
g. master suite
i. study

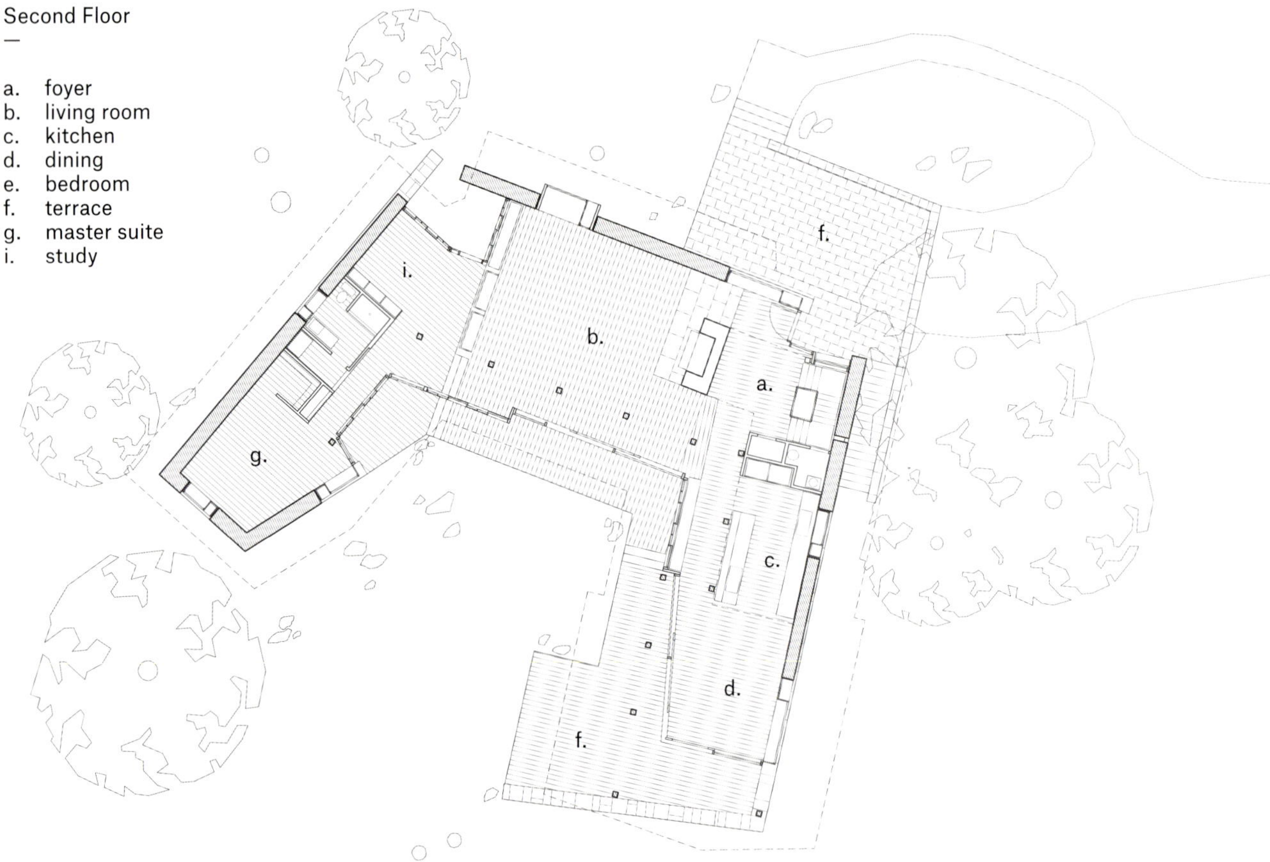

First Floor

—

e. bedroom
f. terrace
h. garage

Tribeca Residence

New York, New York

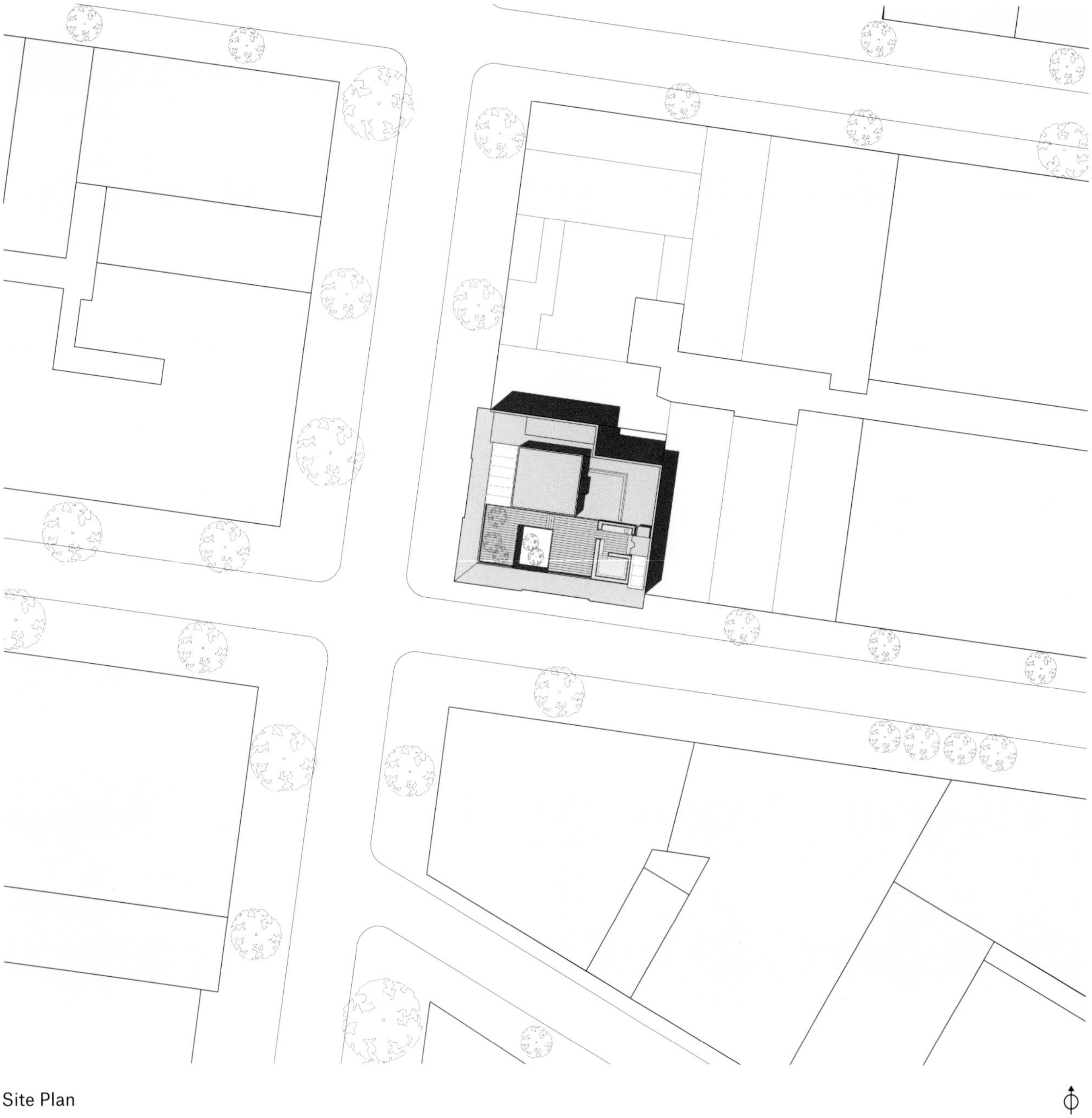

Site Plan

This three-story loft is the primary residence for a New York couple, their four children, and their large extended family. Located within an early-twentieth-century building in Tribeca that has been home to civic and cultural icons throughout its history, the loft comprises the top three levels and rooftop of the ten-story historic structure.

The restored windows on the apartment's historic exterior create an entirely new spatial and material experience in the interior. The design lifts and shifts the floor and ceilings to vary proportions and invite in natural light. Courtyards are carved deep into the spaces, bringing gardens and outdoor space to a residence in lower Manhattan. The multistory interior spaces are unified with a continuous band of cast aluminum panels, resembling book-matched wood or embroidered textile walls. Site-specific works by artists bring kaleidoscopic light and views into the heart of the residence and animate the walls and gardens. In addition to multiple bedroom suites and nanny and chef's quarters, the house includes an indoor gym, a billiards room, fire poles, and secret passages. It is an extraordinary space for entertaining, a world unto itself, with a rooftop deck and garden that provide spectacular views of the city and the Hudson River.

Contemporary Art
Jasper Johns
RARE BIRD OF FASHION
ISABEL TOLEDO
PICASSO

Roof Level/Penthouse

—

a. foyer
f. terrace
h. hot tub

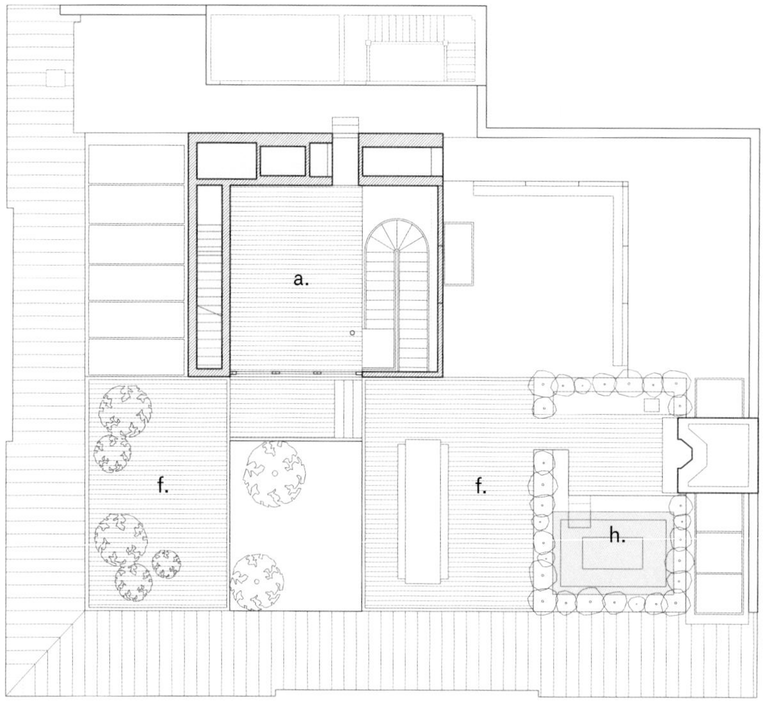

Tenth Floor

—

a. foyer
b. living room
c. kitchen
d. dining
e. bedroom
f. courtyard
g. master suite
i. study
j. gallery

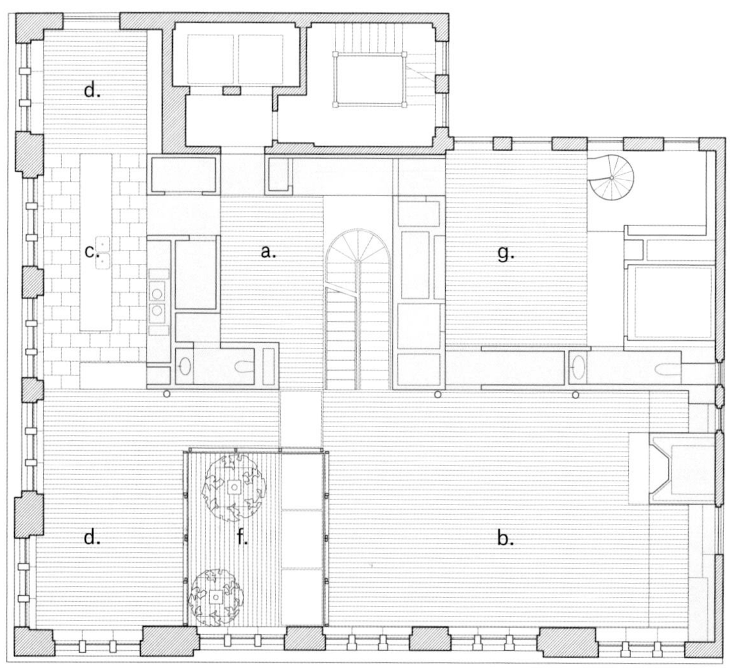

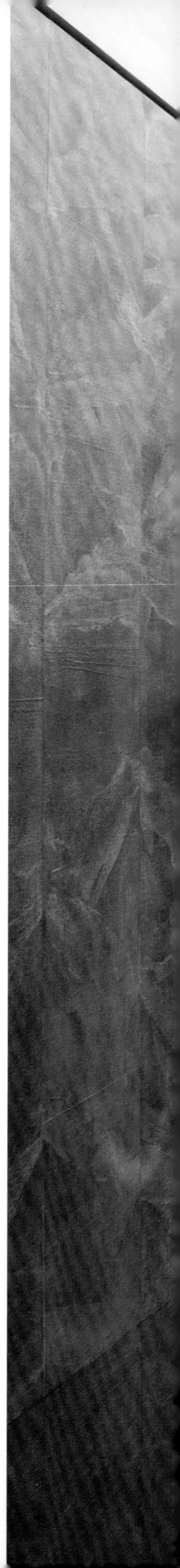

Ninth Floor

—

a. foyer
e. bedroom
i. study
j. gallery
k. dressing

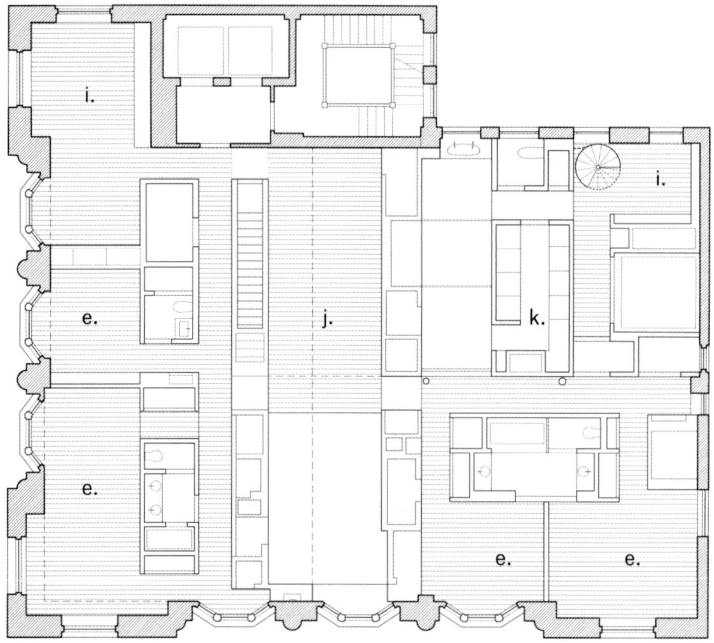

Eighth Floor

—

i. study
l. game room
m. fitness
n. service quarters

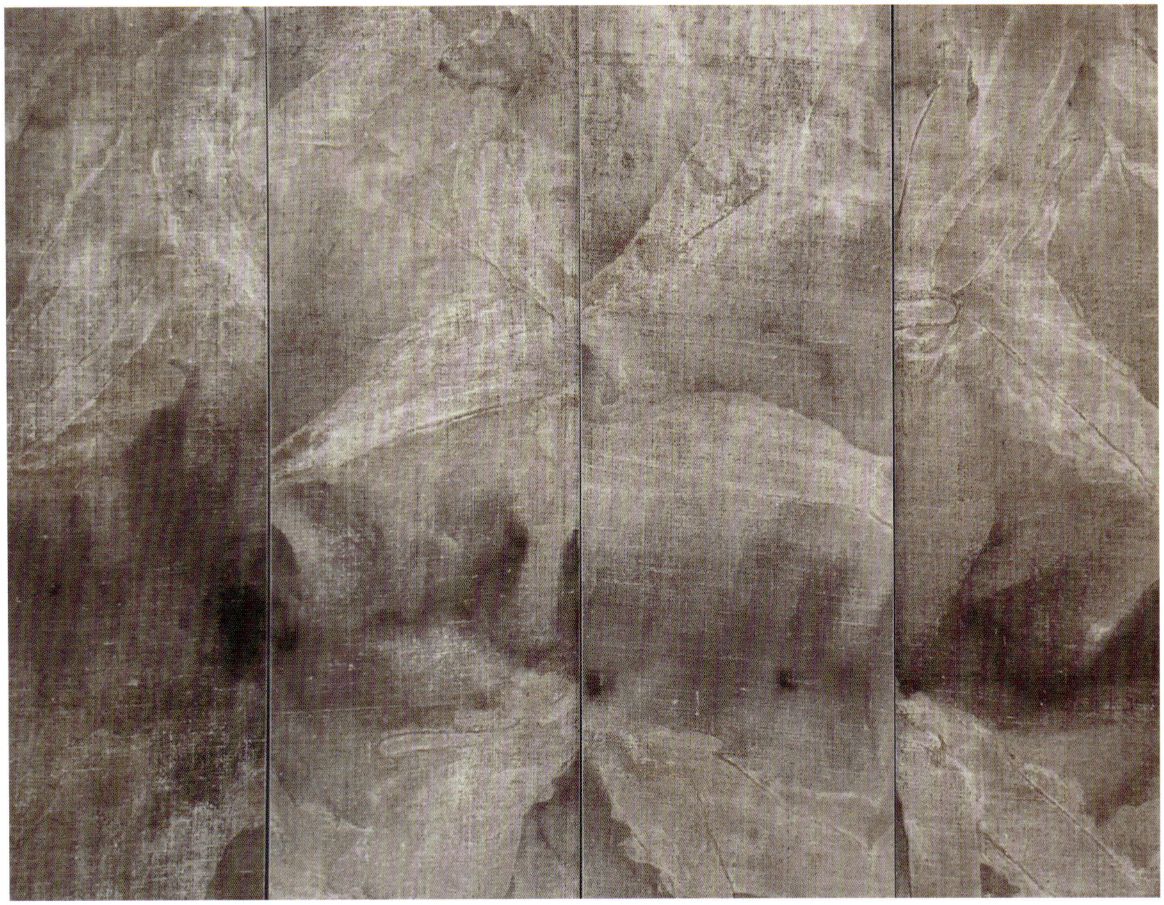

Portland Heights Residence

Portland, Oregon

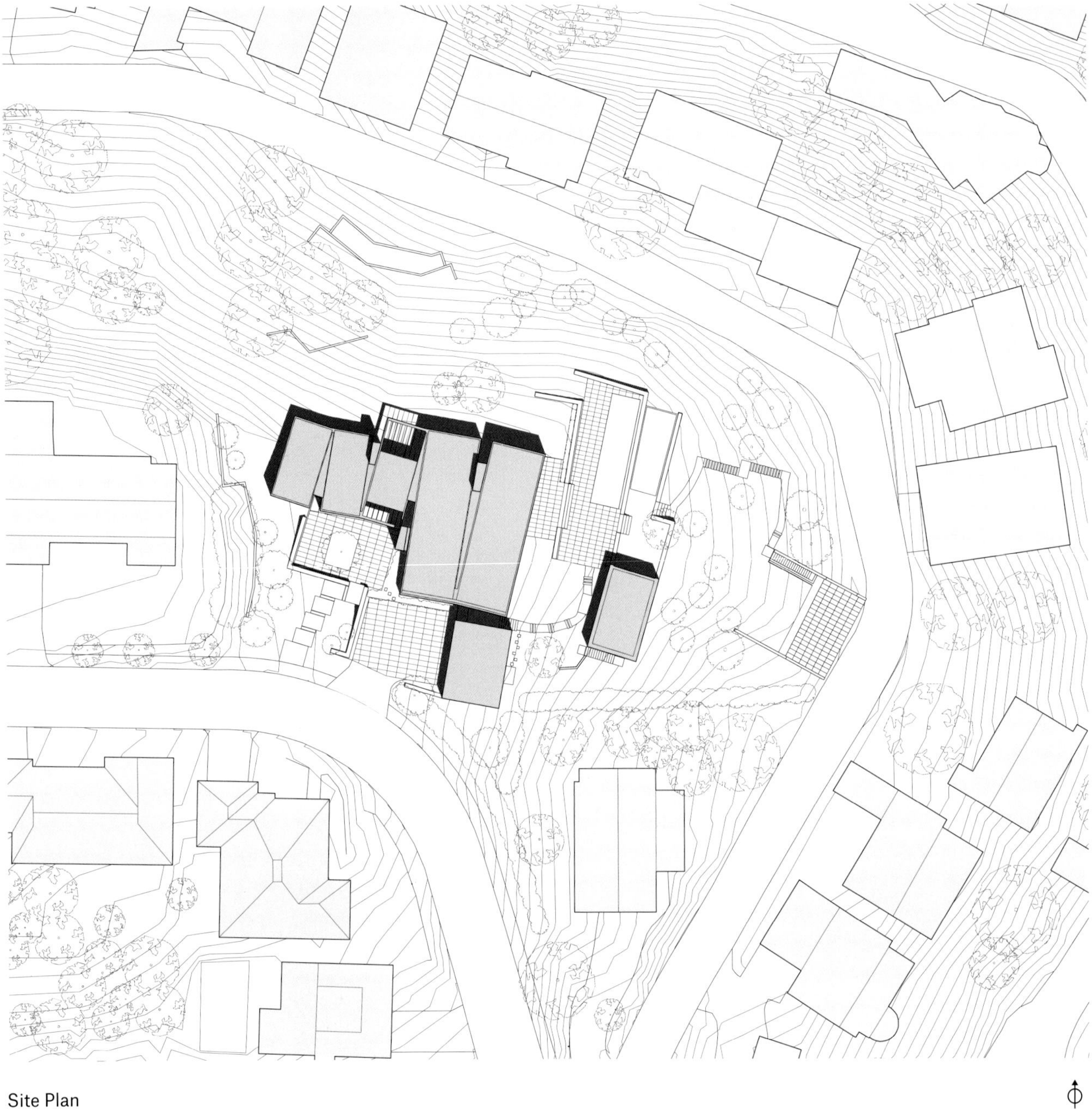

Site Plan

The Portland Heights Residence is sited on a promontory of the Tualatin Mountains with panoramic views of the city and the Cascade Range beyond. Built for a prominent Portland couple and their grown children, the residence includes a main house, a guest house, and two garages—all surrounded by terraced patios, courts, and gardens. The residence occupies its own park within the city, creating a family refuge and ideal place for entertaining.

Constructed of board-form concrete and western red cedar, the main house hinges and unfolds as interconnected pavilions that are joined by concrete hearths and small courtyards. These interstitial courts give focus, warmth, light, and natural ventilation to the interior living spaces. On the main level, the house moves from more intimate spaces, including the master suite and reading room, to larger and more open volumes for formal dining and gathering. Floor-to-ceiling views, operable window walls, and generous balconies give the impression of hovering over the city. Below, bedrooms, recreation rooms, and a swimming pool engage the stepping landscape. Opposite the main terrace, the guest house is a simple rectangular block of native basalt that draws its rugged geometry and material palette from the surrounding garden walls.

MOTHERWELL

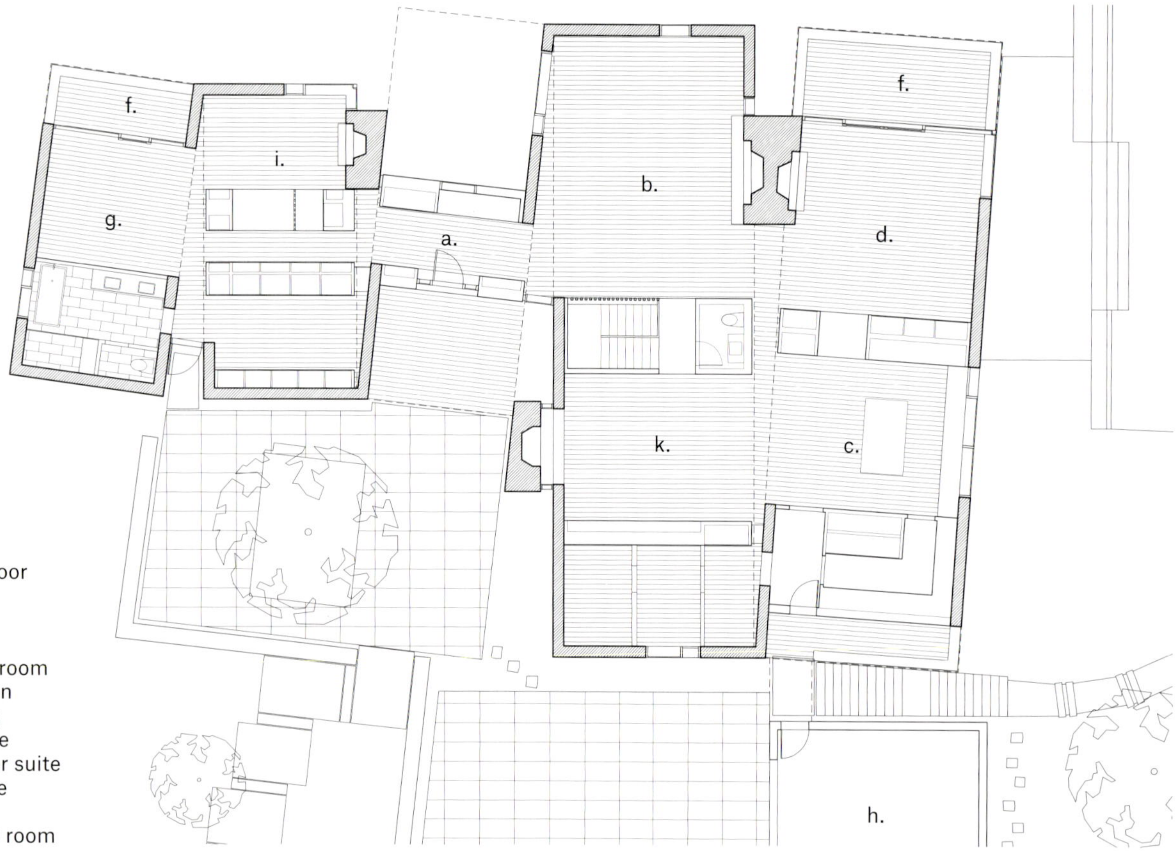

Second Floor

—

a. foyer
b. living room
c. kitchen
d. dining
f. terrace
g. master suite
h. garage
i. study
k. family room

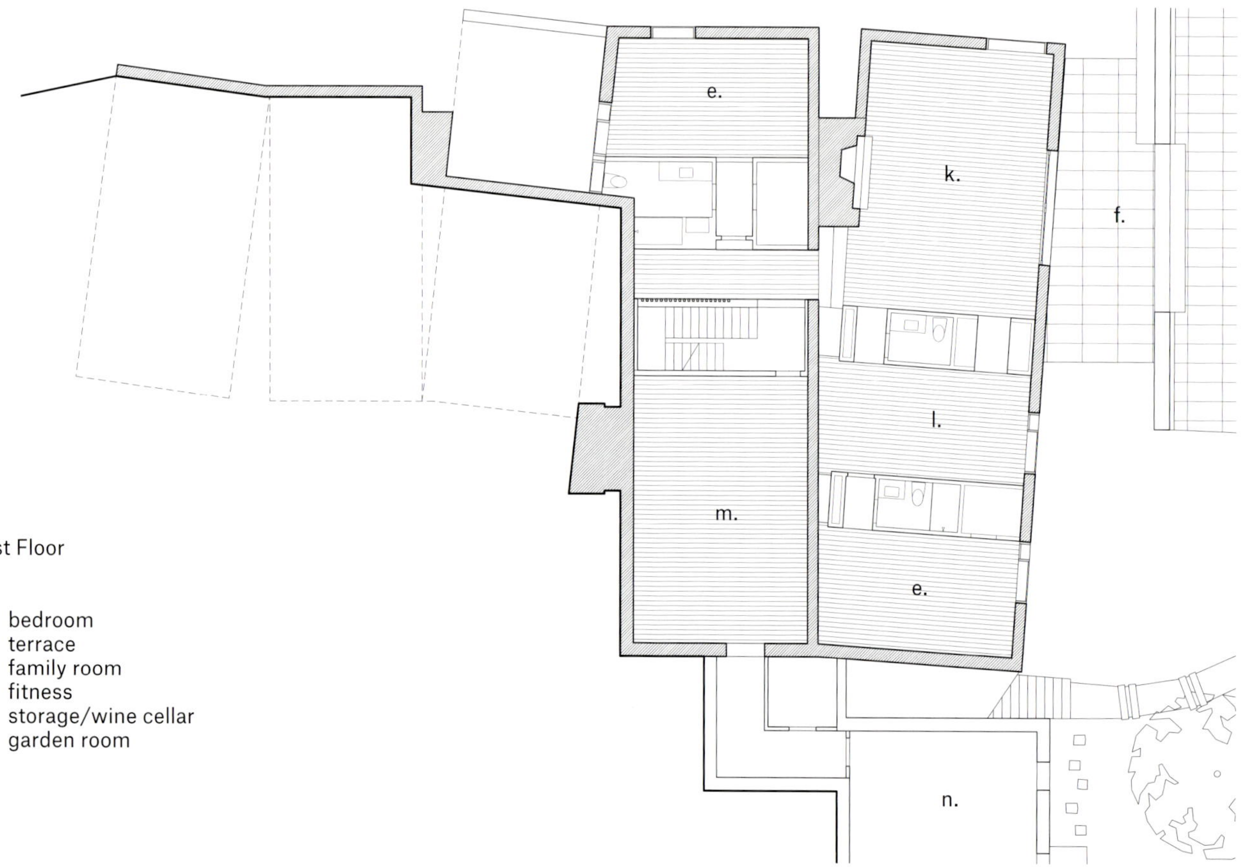

First Floor

—

e. bedroom
f. terrace
k. family room
l. fitness
m. storage/wine cellar
n. garden room

PIGEON

Dutchess County Main Residence

Stanfordville, New York

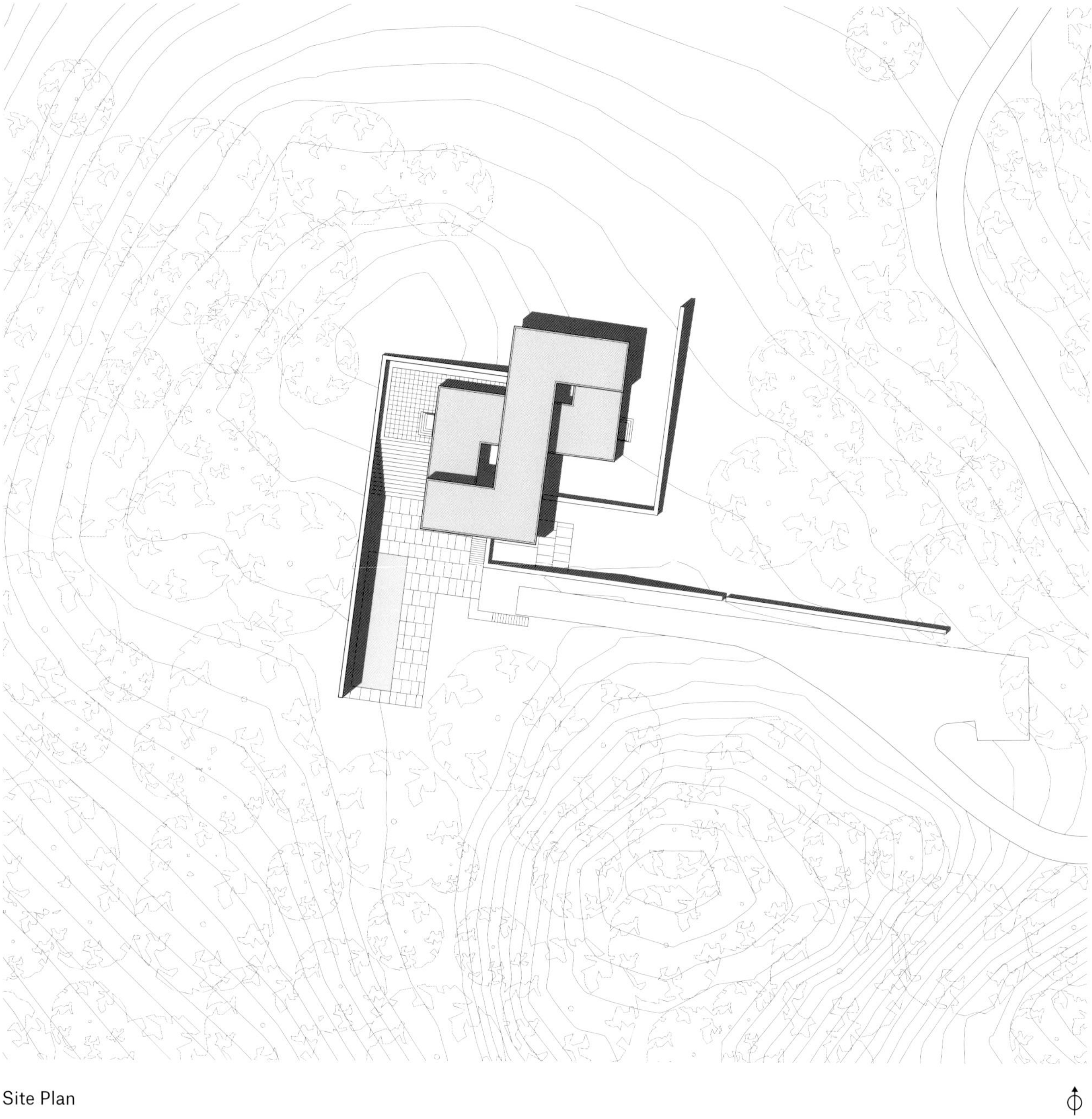

Site Plan

A New York City family with an important contemporary art collection commissioned Allied Works to design a residence, guest house, private gallery, and outbuildings on their estate in Dutchess County, New York. The entire 400-acre property, with its diverse terrain of forests, rolling hills, and open meadows, is now home to site-specific buildings and works of installation art. The main house was the last of these projects to be constructed.

The house is sited on the peak of a hill with panoramic views of the pastoral surroundings and distant Catskill Mountains. Wrapped in expansive panels of etched, translucent, and transparent glass, the main body of the residence takes the form of a two-level helix, linked by double-height volumes and a sculptural central staircase. The building surfaces change with the quality of light, reflecting and dissolving into the landscape. Three terraces of fieldstone and marble anchor the house to the surrounding terrain. The house incorporates many pieces of commissioned art, including etched glass panels by Mel Bochner and a 360-degree video installation by Doug Aitken. The feeling of the residence is one of fluidity and change, revealing new relationships between art, architecture, the land, and the family.

←

Doug Aitken
Light House, 2012

First Floor

—

a. foyer
b. living room
c. kitchen
d. dining
f. terrace
j. library
k. family room
h. pool

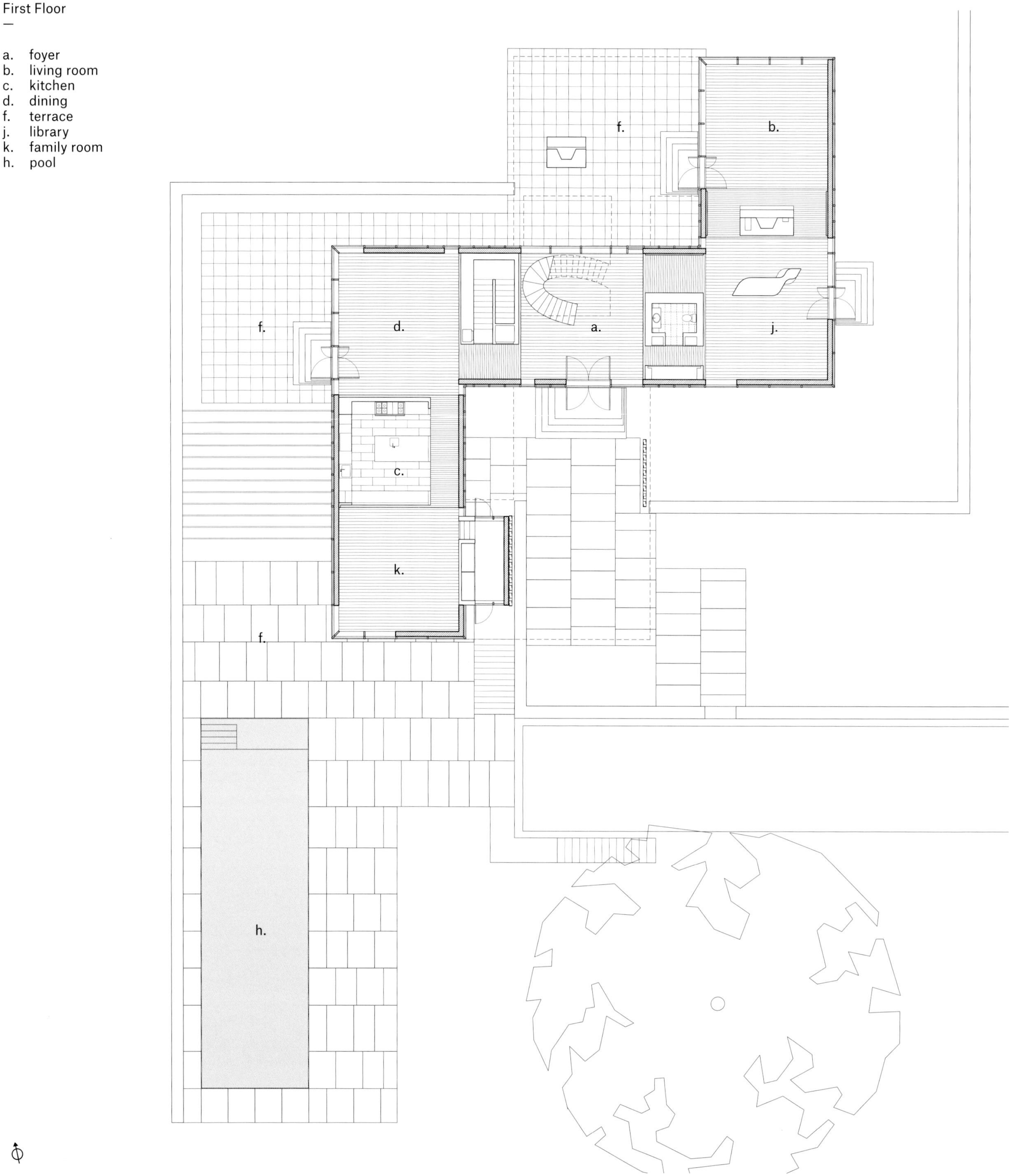

Second Floor

—

e. bedroom
f. terrace
g. master suite
i. studio

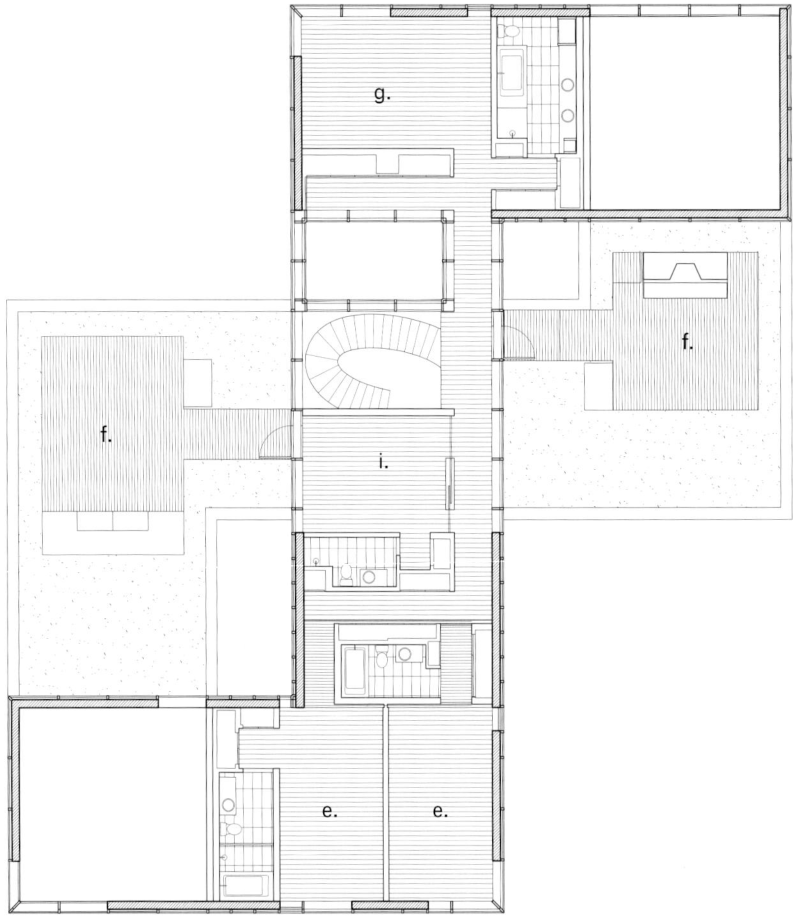

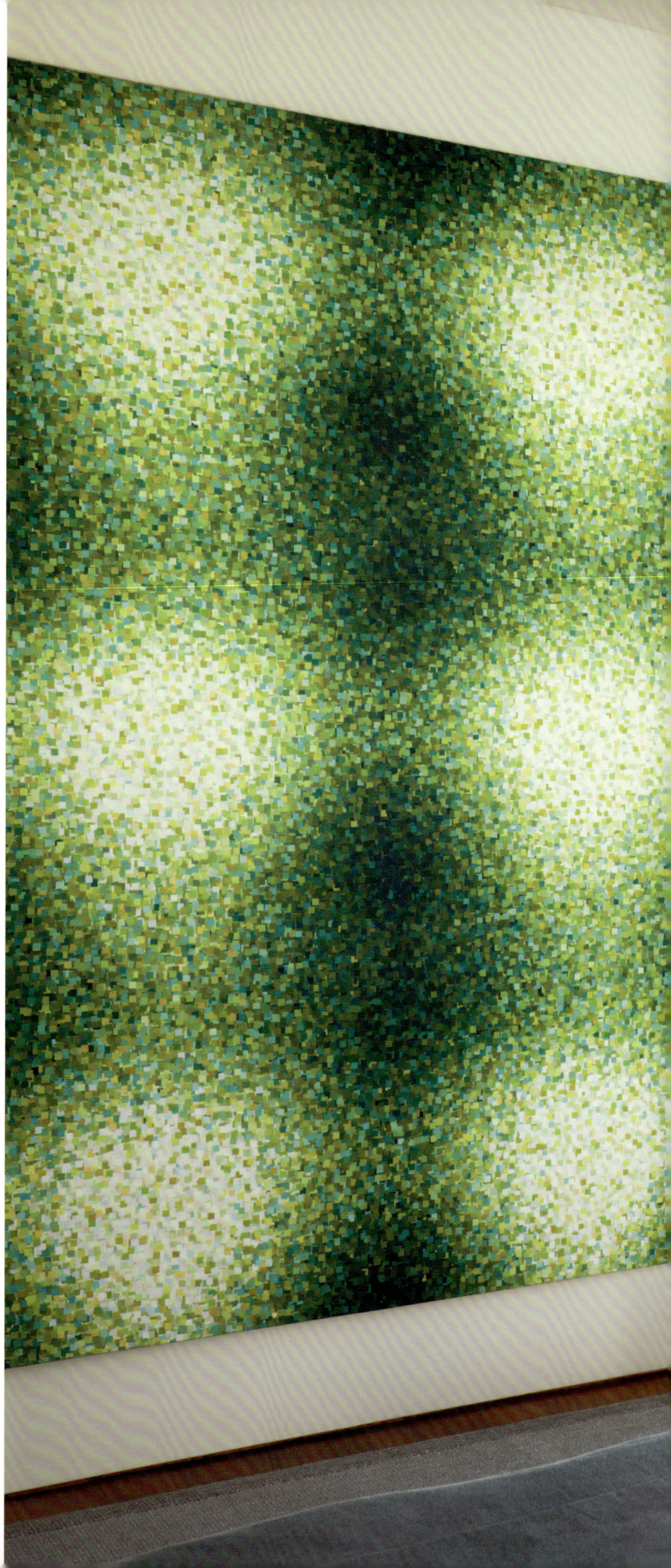

Inhabiting the Frame

——Joseph Becker

"The Architect, by his arrangement of forms, realizes an order which is a pure creation of his spirit; by forms and shapes he affects our senses to an acute degree and provokes plastic emotions; by relationships which he creates he wakes profound echoes in us, he gives us the measure of an order which we feel to be in accordance with that of our world, he determines the various movements of our heart and of our understanding; it is then that we experience the sense of beauty."[1]

——Le Corbusier, *Vers une Architecture* 1923

At the dawn of architecture's Modern movement, Le Corbusier declared that architecture's "raison d'être" was not only one of common practicality, or simply of shelter and structure, but one of emotional and visual resonance. Architecture's most adroit ability, he expressed in his writings, was in eliciting awe. Corbusier was not the first thinker to declare that architecture was much more than the sum of its materials: spaces of spiritual transcendence have existed in parallel with the history of mankind. By virtue of his manifesto, the architect's role in designing spaces that could augment the experience of modern life was articulated as not just an opportunity but a duty. Architecture functions as art does, exploring the capacity to change one's frame of mind, to nourish and comfort, inspire and provoke.

A great architect works to bring structures to fruition that enrich the banal of the everyday with the potential of the rarefied sublime, tapping into the desires of the human experience and fostering a communion between built space and inhabitant. Le Corbusier was expressing that through the distillation of form and material the balance and priorities within architecture could affect our most latent sensibilities, and thus encourage the possibility of becoming emotionally connected to a place, or when amenable, to each other. Allied Works Architecture, founded in 1994 by Brad Cloepfil, has made it their mission to create spaces where this kind of engagement can unfold.

Architecture is fundamentally about organizing a spatial experience, formalized according to needs and desires, program and site, aesthetics and materials, and the less appealing practical concerns such as budgets and code. Where many architects differ from each other is in the weight they give to one motivating force over another, leveraging their artistic vision against the industrial constraints. Allied Works' rich and expanding history of built projects offer more than enough evidence of their dedication to a vision of architecture that prioritizes harmony between the poetic experience of space and its programmatic functionality. Crucially, it is the site—not only the physical and natural environment, but also the cultural and sociological conditions—that tends to inform Cloepfil's work, whose engagement in the reading of a place is an investment that manifests itself in buildings that respond to the range of landscapes they are set in, from the metropolitan to the bucolic. By absorbing these conditions, Allied Works' buildings act to mediate between interiority and exteriority, and between the enclosed and the open. From the vantage of the inhabitant, the architecture's nuanced assemblage gathers isolated moments of the outside, anchoring the buildings through a series of views, narrowing the magnitude of the expanse, using walls and apertures to offer slices of the site that are sized to the interior moments, simultaneously reminding us of our human-ness, of the enormity of the world beyond the window, and the immediacy of the space at hand. The building is a framing apparatus, tuned to its landscape, the movement of light, and the unchoreographed flows of its occupants. Through it, we are invited to enter into the composition, to become actors in the unfolding negotiation between closed and open space.

Cloepfil trusts in architecture's ability to create a microcosm of the larger contexts that affect our lives, and distills them into serene environments that allow us to take our time, processing at our own pace. Each project operates as a platform for engagement, from the domestic and intimate to the public and collective, using scale and volume to form a relationship between the architecture and our physical presence and our mental awareness. As Dean Sobel, director of the Allied Works–designed Clyfford Still Museum notes, Cloepfil's buildings take cues directly from the often meandering movement of people, but even more importantly, each project is driven by the desire to create a "palpable human experience."[2] As intimate spaces, dwellings host a multitude of these heuristic conditions, ranging from the solitary to the social. Homes are sanctuaries for the personal and the familial. They are sites of growth and memory, of contemplation and revelry, elucidating the feelings of protection and coexistence and belonging.

In *The Place of Houses*, the architect Charles Moore identified three key tenets of a dwelling. Allied Works Architecture clearly articulates each of these in their work, through their investigations into the relationships to site, materiality, and behavior. "A house is in delicate balance with its surroundings, and they with it. A good house is a created thing made of many parts economically and meaningfully assembled. It speaks not just of the materials from which it is made, but of the intangible rhythms, spirits, and dreams of people's lives."[3] Habitation, Moore expressed, is a concept that extends from the tangible to the ethereal. Physically, this is manifest as a place "where we can be comfortable," where corporeal senses establish our relationship to space, where we absorb the quality of light, the generosity of volume, the palate of materials, and the acoustic and olfactory affects. Successful synergy among these physical sensibilities can yield a metaphorical space where we "can go beyond where we actually are to wherever our imaginations will transport us."[4] This is architecture's idealized capacity: to anticipate, accommodate, and enhance the range of human activity and inhabitation.

"To dwell implies the establishment of a meaningful relationship between man and a given environment." Christian Norberg-Schulz, in *The Concept of Dwelling*, looked at this dialectic between building and landscape as an "act of identification" that could create "a sense of belonging to a certain place."[5] For Cloepfil, the key to producing the enriched space of a dwelling is in fostering a continuous dialogue with the building site, closely linking the landscape conditions to the form generating process. This means to engage with the landscape proactively—revealing it, pushing against it, and embedding within it—in a negotiation between assimilating and contrasting with the rawness of the coast, the lakeshore, the mountains, or the layered urbanism that the building is set against. Each project takes an opportunity to use the structure to edit vistas and narrow focus, punching apertures through rooms and formally articulating a relationship between the immediate space of the dwelling and the wild space beyond.

In the Sun Valley Residence at the foothills of Idaho's Sawtooth Mountain Range, interlocking concrete volumes are interrupted with generous windows that pull the landscape in. Each one presents a calculated scene of the immediate pastoral or the distant assertive mountain ridges. These slippages pull vistas into the house, cogently uninviting the surrounding neighborhood of ski chalets and swinging its attention to the painterly vestiges of the frontier. The landscape turns from the vast exterior into moments of enclosure, as if the building had reached into the primal and earthen surrounds and pulled some of the natural inside the walled gardens, creating intimacy while the concrete forms tentatively open for swatches of blue sky or a composition of wildflowers.

In the Dutchess County Guest House, in upstate New York, a sequence of volumes perched above a creek are woven together by a steel structure that stretches into the forest of slender deciduous trees, extending past the interior volumes and establishing a mediated exterior. The steel beams float out as if etched lines in a viewfinder, proportioning out moments of riparian landscape and delivering them to the occupants relaxing comfortably inside, where another chorus of details craft our relationship through seamlessly integrated pocket doors, hidden pulls, and camouflaged cabinetry. As one gazes out, the architecture augments the unfolding of seasons and cycles of growth and decay, acting as a counterpoint to the radiance of autumn, the stillness of winter, and the abundance of spring.

Nearly a century ago, Corbusier's dogmatic *Towards an Architecture* elucidated the existing parallels between the role of the artist and the role of the architect. Like art, architecture has the capacity to inspire and transform our relationship with the world and resonate with our emotions. Cloepfil is at the helm of Allied Works, and his devout relationship to art is clear. He investigates across disciplines and collaborates directly with artists, designing buildings that often house remarkable artworks or are ones in themselves. Through his own craft with charcoal and pastel sketches or concept models that act almost as sculpture, his process affords the imagination some leeway—a manifestation of his architectural vision that draws us in. These artifacts embody the essence of the buildings' identity, always in relationship to their site, always exploring a connection of material or form that rationalizes the design decisions. The buildings reveal these efforts, expressing an assertion that there is more than their own static object-ness. Beyond their mediated interiority and their locational logic, these houses are tools for looking—emotional devices that provoke and mesmerize, and optical devices that reveal the natural by juxtaposing it against the built. In them, we inhabit the frame.

---

1 Le Corbusier, *Towards a New Architecture* (New York: Dover Publications, 1985), 1.
2 Dean Sobel and Brad Cloepfil, Brad Cloepfil/Allied Works Architecture: *Case Work: Studies in Form, Space & Construction* (New York: Metropolis Books, 2015), 10.
3 Charles Willard Moore, Gerald Allen, and Donlyn Lyndon, *The Place of Houses*, 1st edition (New York: Holt, Rinehart and Winston, 1974), 49.
4 Ibid.
5 Christian Norberg-Schulz, *The Concept of Dwelling: On the Way to Figurative Architecture*, 1st edition (New York: Rizzoli, 1985), 13.

Joseph Becker is the Associate Curator of Architecture and Design at the San Francisco Museum of Modern Art. Since 2007, Joseph has contributed to over twenty exhibitions at SFMOMA, including curating *Tomás Saraceno: Stillness in Motion—Cloud Cities* (2016–17) and *Field Conditions* (2012) as well as co-curating *Lebbeus Woods, Architect* (2013–14) and *Typeface to Interface: Graphic Design from the Collection* (2016). In addition, he has been responsible for many major acquisitions for SFMOMA's collection as well as the exhibition design and visual direction of the majority of SFMOMA's A+D exhibitions during his decade-long tenure. He has served on numerous architecture, design, and public art panels; been an invited juror at many national architecture programs; led workshops on exhibition and experiential design; moderated public dialogues; and lectured internationally. Becker is also a contributing author to publications in design, art, and architecture, and in 2016 was selected as one of Artsy.net's *20 Most Influential Young Curators in the United States*. He received both his Bachelor of Architecture and his Master of Advanced Architectural Design in Design Theory and Critical Practice from the California College of the Arts, where he has been a Visiting Professor.

Catalog

1998
Winslow Residence
Portland, Oregon

Size—
3,150 s.f. main house
700 s.f. garage
325 s.f. studio

Rooms—
3 bedrooms, 3 bathrooms

Site—
A rolling, pastoral site in the West Hills above Portland, Oregon

Features—
Open plan, custom wood windows and casework, freestanding garage and studio, kitchen garden, terrace and courtyard

1999
Tumalo Residence
Bend, Oregon

Size—
1,200 s.f. addition
700 s.f. renovation

Rooms—
2 bedrooms, 2 bathrooms

Site—
Flat, open meadow near pine forests and the Deschutes River in Central Oregon

Features—
Kitchen and living room additions designed as interconnected pavilions; custom timber framing, cladding and casework; living spaces and exterior terraces lifted above grade to reduce impact on sensitive site

2000
Blue Lake Residence
Sisters, Oregon
——p. 124

Size—
4,300 s.f.

Rooms—
5 bedrooms, 3.5 bathrooms

Site—
A sloping, wooded site on a 90-acre property overlooking Blue Lake, in the Cascade Range of central Oregon

Features—
Native stone perimeter walls, heavy timber frame, reclaimed Douglas-fir structure and paneling, cedar cladding, floor-to-ceiling windows and sliding doors, exterior terraces

Collaborators—
Structral: Ang Engineering Group
Landscape: Michael Schultz
Timber: Earthwood Custom Framing
Stonework: Kevin Spencer Masonry
Contractor: Construction Management Services, Chuck Newport & Paul Spezza

Glisan Street Residence
Portland, Oregon
——p. 108

Size—
3,500 s.f. residence
(14,000 s.f total building area)

Rooms—
4 bedrooms, 3.5 bathrooms

Site—
Historic Alphabet District of Portland; residential, commercial, and mixed-use structures dating from 1890s to present day

Features—
Floor-to-ceiling glazing, woven wire mesh ventilator panels, slate cladding, exterior terraces, roof garden with fireplace

Collaborators—
Structural: Ang Engineering Group
Contractor: Algonquin Construction

2003
Willapa Bay Residence
Ocean Park, Washington
——p. 94

Size—
3,500 s.f.

Rooms—
3 bedrooms, 3 bathrooms

Site—
Coastal meadow facing Willapa Bay, on the eastern edge of Washington's Long Beach Peninsula

Features—
Expressed timber structure, freestanding studio/workshop, darkroom, floor-to-ceiling windows and sliding doors, kitchen garden, exterior terraces

Collaborators—
Structural: Ang Engineering Group
Landscape: Green Angel
Contractor: W&E Construction

2004
Sun Valley Residence
Ketchum, Idaho
——p. 46

Size—
4,500 s.f.

Rooms—
4 bedrooms, 3.5 bathrooms

Site—
Residential neighborhood on the outskirts of Ketchum; located in a rolling meadow of native grasses and wildflowers

Features—
Seamless sitecast concrete wall and fireplaces, private landscape courts, event terrace and lawn, floor-to-ceiling glazing, custom metalwork gates and garden walls

Collaborators—
Landscape: Lutsko Associates Landscape
Lighting: Horton Lees Brogden
Interior Design: Easton Moss & Co
Structural: KPFF
Contractor: Dembergh Construction

Council Crest Residence
Portland, Oregon

Size—
650 s.f. addition
1,250 s.f. renovation

Rooms—
3 bedrooms, 4 bathrooms

Site—
Historic 1938 home and former residence of Pietro Belluschi, located on a wooded, sloping site near Portland's Council Crest Park

Features—
New master suite with exterior decks and floor-to-ceiling glazing, garden terrace, new kitchen, dining area and casework

Collaborators—
Structural: KPFF
Contractor: Don Tankersley & Co.

2007
Skyline Residence
Portland, Oregon

Size—
6,000 s.f. main house
1,300 s.f. studio/garage

Rooms—
4 bedrooms, 4 bathrooms

Site—
Forest clearing in the Tualatin Mountains, overlooking the Columbia River

Features—
Continuous, low-slope roof, cascading exterior terraces, pool, library, indoor/outdoor fireplace, music and movement studio

Dutchess County Guest House
Dutchess County, New York
——p. 26

Size—
1,300 s.f.

Rooms—
2 bedrooms, 2 bathrooms

Site—
400-acre estate in the Hudson River Valley; the guest house occupies a heavily wooded site on the banks of a neighboring creek, near the eastern edge of the property

Features—
Continuous, cantilevered, expressed structural steel frame, mahogany paneling, stone tile and hearth, floor-to-ceiling windows, exterior terraces

Collaborators—
Building Envelope: R.A Heintges Architects
Structural: R.A. Silman
Interiors: Studio Frazar
Landscape: Michael Van Valkenburgh Associates
Contractor: Berkshire Wilton Partners

Macleay View Residence
Portland, Oregon

Size—
4,400 s.f.

Rooms—
3 bedrooms, 3.5 bathrooms

Site—
Compact, 40-degree sloped site in Raleigh Hills neighborhood, with views of downtown Portland, the Willamette River, and the Cascade Range

Features—
Vertical, three-story configuration with open central atrium and stair; elevator services all levels, custom masonry and wood casement windows, masonry exterior and fireplace, exterior terraces on all levels, soaking tub and outdoor shower

Collaborators—
Contractor: Don Tankersley & Co.
Interiors: Jennifer Fowler Interiors
Project Advisors: Studio Jay

2009
Tribeca Residence
New York, New York
——p. 138

Size—
13,300 s.f.

Rooms—
5 bedrooms, 5.5 bathrooms

Site—
Upper floors and roof terrace of a landmarked 1921 mixed-use building in Manhattan, within the Tribeca West Historic District

Features—
Cast aluminum interior wall panels, integrated courtyards and gardens, roof terrace, site-specific art installations by Doug Aitken and Paula Hayes

Collaborators—
Landscape: Paula Hayes
Artist: Doug Aitken
Aluminum Panels: Polich Tallix
Interiors: Jarlath Mellet
Structural: Silman
Contractor: Taocon

Portland Heights Residence:
Portland, Oregon
——p. 158

Size—
8,300 s.f. main residence
700 s.f. guest house
1,500 s.f. garage

Rooms—
4 bedrooms, 5.5 bathrooms

Site—
West Hills/Portland Heights neighborhood of Portland, Oregon; residence is sited on a projecting ridge that offers 180 degree views of the Cascade Range, the Willamette River, and the city below

Features—
Basalt stonework, board-formed concrete structure and certified Western Red Cedar cladding, freestanding guest house, kitchen garden, event terrace and pool

Collaborators—
Interior Design: Studio Frazar
Landscape: Pivot Landscape
Architecture & Sean Hogan
Structural: KPFF
Contractor: Don Tankersley & Co.

2010
Big Sky Residence
Billings, Montana

Size—
2,650 s.f. renovation
800 s.f. new construction

Rooms—
4 bedrooms, 2.5 bathrooms

Site—
Residential neighborhood in Billings, Montana, between the Bluffs and the Yellowstone River

Features—
New master suite, entry foyer, custom wood casement windows and doors, exterior terraces and shade trellises

Collaborators—
Structural: Krivonen Associates
Contractor: Turning Leaf Construction

2011
Neskowin Beach House
Neskowin, Oregon
——p. 74

Size—
1,550 s.f.

Rooms—
3 bedrooms, 2 bathrooms

Site—
A small residential enclave located on wooded, steeply sloping hillside above the central Oregon coast

Features—
Board and batten Western Red Cedar exterior siding, Douglas-fir interior wall paneling, operable interior partitions, roof terrace

Collaborators—
Structural: Madden & Baughman
Contractor: Joe Goodrich

2012
Dutchess County Main Residence
Dutchess County, New York
——p. 184

Size:—
5,500 s.f.

Rooms—
3 bedrooms, 4.5 bathrooms

Site—
400-acre estate in the Hudson River Valley; house occupies a site along a ridge at the head of a large meadow, providing sweeping views of the estate and mountains beyond

Features—
Custom steel-and-glass curtain wall, stone retaining walls, interior and exterior fireplaces, exterior terraces and swimming pool, site-specific art installations by Mel Bochner and Doug Aitken

Collaborators—
Landscape: Michael Van Valkenburgh & Associates
Interior Design: Studio Frazar
Structural: Silman
Artist: Doug Aitken Workshop
Art Projection: Worldstage
Contractor: Berkshire Wilton Partners

2014
Fairmount Residence
Portland, Oregon
(design)

Size—
6,000 s.f. main house
1,100 s.f. studio/garage

Rooms—
3 bedrooms, 3 bathrooms

Site—
Sloped, south-facing ridgeline in Portland's West Hills

Features—
Continuous, low-slope roof form, native stone site and building walls, commercial grade kitchen, living, dining room and hearth are configured to accommodate lectures, events and meetings for local nonprofits

Collaborators—
Structural: KPFF
Arborist: Whole Tree Works

2016
Bridgehampton Residence
Bridgehampton, New York
(design)

Size—
3,000 s.f.

Rooms—
2 bedrooms, 2.5 bathrooms

Site—
Residential neighborhood on Long Island, set within agricultural fields, tidal estuaries, and hardwood groves

Features—
Continuous, low-slope metal roofing, custom exterior and interior wood cladding and casework, indoor/outdoor fireplace, exposed timber framing, covered, exterior dining terrace, swimming pool, changing room and outdoor bar

Acknowledgments

This body of work, these residences and retreats, would not be possible without our clients. Their vision, their passion, and their patronage have allowed us to explore the possibilities of building and dwelling and the profound relationship between land, life, and craft. Each site, family, and individual has been a pleasure to encounter and to work with; over the years, I believe these experiences and relationships have energized and re-focused our entire practice. For these gifts, and your friendship, I would like to offer each of you my deep thanks and gratitude.

Next up, this book—as its own act of design and making—is a project we have long envisioned, and have waited for the opportunity to do it properly. First I would like to thank Ron Broadhurst and his team at Rizzoli for their interest in our work and commitment to the project, and also for their insight into the content and composition of the completed artifact. I also want to acknowledge the work of Brian Walbergh, our book designer and resident expert on graphics, typography, and all things printed. As the engine and creative lead of Allied Print Works, he's brought new rigor and clarity to our identity and expression.

Finally, to my many dedicated colleagues at Allied Works, past and present, who have made these houses, and all that we create, come together so beautifully. It has truly been an honor to work with you all.

—Brad Cloepfil

About Allied Works

Allied Works is a collective design office focusing on architecture, decorative arts, and information and graphic design. The firm was established to engage artists, builders, thinkers, and diverse professionals in a more comprehensive creative conversation. It is an effort that continues to inspire us and inform our work. Within our expanded practice are four integrated disciplines: Allied Works Architecture creates buildings, sites, and spaces; Allied Info Works produces media, experiential, and information-based works; Allied Form Works explores craft-based and human-scaled projects, including artworks, installations, and furniture design; and Allied Print Works designs and produces diverse publications and printed matter.

We endeavor to create projects that are singular and specific to each client, set of conditions, and project type. Our work is broad by intention; we do not approach any project with a preconceived agenda or style, but rather as a new beginning, grounded in the beauty and character of place, the unique possibilities of experience, and the values and aspirations of our clients.

Notable projects include the Wieden+Kennedy World Headquarters in Portland, the Museum of Arts and Design in New York City, the Clyfford Still Museum in Denver, the Sokol Blosser Winery in Dayton, Oregon, and the National Music Centre of Canada in Calgary, Alberta. Forthcoming projects include the National Veterans Memorial Museum in Columbus, Ohio, and the redesign of Eleven Madison Park, a Michelin three-star restaurant in Manhattan.

↓ Maryhill Overlook, Goldendale, Washington

First published in the United States of America in 2017 by
Rizzoli International Publications, Inc.

300 Park Avenue South
New York, NY 10010
www.rizzoliusa.com

ISBN: 978-0-8478-6032-6
LCCN: 2017944936

Book Design—
Brian Walbergh, Allied Print Works

Typeface—
ITC Garamond & Atlas Grotesk

Plans—
Site Plans: Reproduced at 1:800
Floor Plans: Reproduced at 1:240

Printed and bound in China

2017 2018 2019 2020 2021 / 10 9 8 7 6 5 4 3 2 1

Cover Image—
Dutchess County Main Residence from afar
Photo: Jeremy Bittermann

Photo credits—
Hélène Binet: pp. 12, 19, 34, 37, 40, 41, 43, 44, 47, 49, 52, 53, 94, 97, 98, 100, 101, 103–107, 116, 120, 122
Jeremy Bittermann: pp. 14,15, 16, 20, 29, 30, 33, 38, 42, 55–57, 61–70, 75, 78,80–92, 159, 162, 164–181, 182, 186, 188–193, 195, 208
Marion Brenner: pp. 50, 72
Brad Cloepfil: pp. 10, 22, 71, 77, 127, 137, 155
John Dimaio: pp. 128, 131, 134–136
Scott Frances: pp. 142, 144, 149, 150–154
Arthur Hitchcock: pp. 10
Dean Kaufman: pp. 18, 27, 139, 146, 156
Daniel Mihalyo: pp. 10
reproduced with permission of the artist, from:
Mihalyo, Daniel. *Wood Burners*. New York: Princeton Architectural Press, 1997.
Jason Schmidt: pp. 23, 185, 194, 196, 199, 201-207
Sally Schoolmaster: pp. 108, 112, 114, 115, 117, 118, 125, 132, 223
Brian Walbergh: pp. 111, 161
Xuancheng Zhu: pp. 141